CHURCH ELDERS

9Marks: Building Healthy Churches

Edited by Mark Dever and Jonathan Leeman

Expositional Preaching: How We Speak God's Word Today, David Helm

Sound Doctrine: How a Church Grows in the Love and Holiness of God, Bobby Jamieson

The Gospel: How the Church Portrays the Beauty of Christ, Ray Ortlund

Evangelism: How the Whole Church Speaks of Jesus, J. Mack Stiles

Church Membership: How the World Knows Who Represents Jesus, Jonathan Leeman

Church Discipline: How the Church Protects the Name of Jesus, Jonathan Leeman

Church Elders: How to Shepherd God's People Like Jesus, Jeramie Rinne

BUILDING HEALTHY CHURCHES

CHURCH ELDERS

HOW TO
SHEPHERD
GOD'S
PEOPLE LIKE
JESUS

JERAMIE RINNE

WHEATON, ILLINOIS

Church Elders: How to Shepherd God's People Like Jesus

Copyright © 2014 by Jeramie Rinne

Published by Crossway
    1300 Crescent Street
    Wheaton, Illinois 60187

Cover design: Dual Identity inc.

Cover image(s): Wayne Brezinka for brezinkadesign.com

First printing 2014

Printed in the United States of America

Unless otherwise indicated, Scripture quotations are from *The Holman Christian Standard Bible*®. Copyright © 1999, 2000, 2002, 2003 by Holman Bible Publishers. Used by permission.

Scripture quotations marked ESV are from the ESV® Bible (The Holy Bible, English Standard Version®), copyright © 2001 by Crossway. 2011 Text Edition. Used by permission. All rights reserved.

Scripture quotations marked KJV are from the *King James Version* of the Bible.

All emphases in Scripture quotations have been added by the author.

Trade paperback ISBN: 978-1-4335-4087-5
ePub ISBN: 978-1-4335-4090-5
PDF ISBN: 978-1-4335-4088-2
Mobipocket ISBN: 978-1-4335-4089-9

Library of Congress Cataloging-in-Publication Data

Rinne, Jeramie, 1970–
   Church Elders : how to shepherd God's people like Jesus / Jeramie Rinne.
      pages cm.— (9Marks: building healthy churches)
     Includes bibliographical references and index.
     ISBN 978-1-4335-4087-5 (hc)
     1. Elders (Church officers) 2. Christian leadership.
I. Title.
BV680.R56   2014
253—dc23   2013024164

Crossway is a publishing ministry of Good News Publishers.

LB			24	23	22	21	20	19	18	17
16	15	14	13	12	11	10	9	8	7	

To the elders of South Shore Baptist Church,
my band of brothers

CONTENTS

SERIES PREFACE

Do you believe it's your responsibility to help build a healthy church? If you are a Christian, we believe that it is.

Jesus commands you to make disciples (Matt. 28:18–20). Jude says to build yourselves up in the faith (Jude 20–21). Peter calls you to use your gifts to serve others (1 Pet. 4:10). Paul tells you to speak the truth in love so that your church will become mature (Eph. 4:13, 15). Do you see where we are getting this?

Whether you are a church member or leader, the Building Healthy Churches series of books aims to help you fulfill such biblical commands and so play your part in building a healthy church. Another way to say it might be, we hope these books will help you grow in loving your church like Jesus loves your church.

9Marks plans to produce a short, readable book on each of what Mark has called nine marks of a healthy church, plus one more on sound doctrine. Watch for books on expositional preaching, biblical theology, the gospel, conversion, evangelism, church membership, church discipline, discipleship and growth, and church leadership.

Local churches exist to display God's glory to the nations. We do that by fixing our eyes on the gospel of Jesus Christ, trusting him for salvation, and then loving one another with

God's own holiness, unity, and love. We pray the book you are holding will help.

With hope,
Mark Dever and Jonathan Leeman
Series editors

INTRODUCTION

"I'm an elder. Now what?"

Many pastors could write a book entitled "What They Didn't Tell Me in Seminary about Pastoral Ministry." That book would probably have some painful, heavy chapters, such as "How to Survive an Ugly Business Meeting" or "What to Say at the Funeral for a Three-Year-Old." Pastoral ministry involves forms of suffering, discouragement, and heartbreak for which no school can prepare a man.

But ministry also holds happy surprises. No one in seminary told me that I would fall in love with my congregation or that I would have a front-row seat to watch God's faithfulness and the gospel's power at work in people's lives.

And no one tipped me off about the joy and satisfaction I would receive from working with lay elders.

I love lay elders.[1] I am awed by men who, despite demanding work schedules and busy home lives, sacrifice time and money, tears and prayers to lead their local churches. I love watching them wrestle together through challenges, make mistakes, and mature in the process. It is like hanging out with the twelve disciples: ordinary, flawed men fulfilling an extraordinary calling by God's grace. The elders in my congregation have truly been a band of brothers for me; I cannot imagine ministry without my fellow shepherds.

I love elders for another reason: they are God's plan for leading his churches. God has always provided shepherds for his people. He gave Moses, Samuel, and the judges to Israel. He raised up Israel's shepherd *par excellence*, King David. And yet, all these men, including David, failed in one way or another. The kings after David increasingly led God's flock into idolatry and injustice. And so the prophets began to speak of a coming shepherd, a new "David" (for example, Isa. 9:1–7; Ezek. 34:20–24).

God made good on his promise by sending Jesus, the Son of David, the Good Shepherd who laid down his life for the sheep and rose again. But it did not stop there. Jesus gave apostles and then *elders* to tend his flock as under-shepherds until he returns (Eph. 4:7–13; 1 Pet. 5:1–4). Elders are Jesus's assistants for shepherding his churches.

GODLY, WELL-INTENTIONED, AND . . . CONFUSED

As much as I love elders for these reasons, I have noticed a recurring problem. Though elders are typically godly and well-intentioned, they are often confused about what being an elder entails. They don't always have a complete grasp of what they are supposed to *do*. And, to be honest, we paid pastors often share their confusion.

Consequently, elders tend to import other leadership paradigms into church oversight, typically drawing from their own experiences and careers. Without a clear, biblical job description for elders, these men naturally fall back on what they know. They assume eldering is like:

- Administering a school
- Running a company
- Commanding a warship
- Managing a project
- Directing operations
- Overseeing subcontractors
- Serving on a board of trustees

Aspects of these life experiences always prove useful in elder leadership. Yet overseeing a church is a unique task.

"I'M AN ELDER. NOW WHAT?"

This book is intended to provide a concise, biblical job description for elders. I wanted to create an easy-to-read, inspiring summary of the elder task that could be given to a new or potential elder who needs to know what an elder is and does. I hope the book will answer a godly, well-intentioned man who asks: "I'm an elder. Now what?"

But this book is not just for current or aspiring elders. It's also for church members. The whole congregation needs to understand God's plan for the local church, including his plan for leadership. Church members can be just as confused about an elder's job description as the elders are.

So I pray that this book will bring health to congregations as members and leaders unify around a biblical vision for ministry and leadership in the local church. I hope that spiritually lethargic, pew-warming Christian men might read this book and experience an awakening desire to shepherd their families and churches. Finally, I'm praying God will use this little book to change the course of a few men's lives by calling them into pastoral ministry as a vocation.

ELDERS, OVERSEERS, AND PASTORS

A quick word about vocabulary: I will be using the terms *elder* and *overseer* interchangeably because the New Testament uses them interchangeably.[2] The eldership is one job with two titles.

Well, actually there are three titles. I will argue in chapter 2 that the term *pastor* (i.e., "shepherd") refers to the same church position as *elder* and *overseer*. Biblically speaking, elders are pastors, who are overseers. The person in a church we typically call a "pastor" is a paid elder, and the person in a church we typically call an "elder" or "overseer" is an unpaid, lay pastor.

Elder or shepherd, overseer or pastor, paid or volunteer. It's all the same job. *But what is that job?* What are elders supposed to do in a local church? What are Jesus's marching orders for his under-shepherds? How do they know if they are completing the mission?

Before we answer those questions, we must do something more basic. We need to understand the biblical qualifications for being an elder. If you are considering taking on the office of elder, your first task is to discern whether you are ready!

1

DON'T ASSUME

I became a disciple of Jesus as a preteen through the faithful gospel ministry of a little elder-led Baptist church outside of Las Vegas, Nevada. At age twenty-six, I became the senior pastor (or senior elder, you could say) of a little Baptist church in the suburbs of Boston, Massachusetts. So you might assume I understood what elders are all about. But believe it or not, it was only *after* I became an elder that I started really studying what the Bible says about elders.

When I did, two things surprised me. First, I was amazed at *how much* the Bible has to say. Almost all of the New Testament authors address elders. There are more than a dozen texts. It became clear to me that Christlike elders are not an optional church feature; they are central to God's plan for shepherding his churches. How had I missed it?

Second, I was startled by *how different* both the biblical job description and the qualifications for elders are from what I had assumed. I had thought I was qualified to be a pastor and elder because I loved Jesus, had a seminary degree, and could preach decently. What more does it take?

Maybe you assume you should be an elder too, but for different reasons. Perhaps you believe the time has come for you to join the elder board because you have been a faithful church member. You have served two terms on the missions committee, hosted a home Bible study, and even taught second-grade Sunday school when they couldn't find a teacher. You have paid your dues, and now it is your turn to lead.

Or maybe you assume you are elder board-bound because you make large donations. The church would not have ended the fiscal year in the black without the check you wrote. Big donors deserve to have a big say and sit on the big boards. Those are the rules. Besides, your church could use a leader with a little business sense.

It is also possible you think you should lead in the church because you lead outside the church. Maybe you manage a successful company, sit on the board of a nonprofit, chair a department, command a battalion, or coach a team. It's safe to assume your leadership skills, experience, and gifting make you an ideal elder candidate.

Right?

As I noted in the introduction, your first elder-related duty is to investigate whether you should in fact be an elder, based on the Bible's qualifications. Don't assume. Even if you have served as an elder before, allow God's Word to vet your candidacy.

Below are six elder qualifications gathered from the New Testament. Read through them prayerfully. Stop and reflect often. Invite others into the conversation. Show this section to your wife, some friends, or an elder, and ask, "Do these qualifications describe me?"

YOU KNOW YOU'RE QUALIFIED TO SERVE AS AN ELDER IF . . .

1. You Want to Be an Elder

In one of the New Testament's longest teachings about elders, the apostle Paul began by saying, "This saying is trustworthy: 'If anyone aspires to be an overseer, he desires a noble work'" (1 Tim. 3:1). Peter put it this way: "Shepherd God's flock among you, not overseeing out of compulsion but freely, according to God's will" (1 Pet. 5:2).

Aspiration. Desire. Freedom. You've got to want it. Faithful shepherding demands much of you. If you don't have an inner hunger for the role, you can burn out. Of course, that doesn't mean that everyone who wants to be an elder is qualified. But it does mean a lack of desire is a problem.

There is a man in my church who is solid elder material. Our nominating team asked him to serve as an elder. In fact, we asked him three times. Apparently the third time was the charm because he finally consented. But as I talked with him more, it became apparent he lacked a strong desire to be an elder. He had agreed to serve in part because he had turned the offer down twice before. Finally, a sense of duty to his church compelled him to agree to serve—the very thing Peter warned against.

He also told me about his desire to free up time in his schedule in order to engage his neighbors and town with the gospel. I could only imagine his likely frustration if he invested himself in shepherding the flock when he longed to be out adding to the flock. So after further prayer, he changed his mind and courageously declined the nomination a third time. We had almost confused an evangelist for an elder.

While not all motivations are godly, you must have an inner desire to be an elder. Has the Holy Spirit placed a godly yearning in your heart to shepherd the local church? What is motivating you?

2. You Exemplify Godly Character

You might assume that the most important characteristic for an elder would be skill in running an organization. While management ability is a part of being a church overseer, the New Testament writers put far greater emphasis on holy character. Jesus's under-shepherds must reflect Jesus's character. Better a godly elder with mediocre leadership gifts than a charismatic leader with glaring moral flaws.

Read over these portions of two overseer qualification lists from Paul. These virtues should fit an elder like a custom-tailored suit:

> An overseer, therefore, must be above reproach, the husband of one wife, self-controlled, sensible, respectable, hospitable, an able teacher, not addicted to wine, not a bully but gentle, not quarrelsome, not greedy. (1 Tim. 3:2–3)

> For an overseer, as God's administrator, must be blameless, not arrogant, not hot-tempered, not addicted to wine, not a bully, not greedy for money, but hospitable, loving what is good, sensible, righteous, holy, self-controlled. (Titus 1:7–8)

Given the importance of Christlike character, let's slow down and consider a few of these qualities in more detail.

Above reproach. Paul began his virtue lists with "above reproach" and "blameless." These descriptions don't mean an elder has transcended sin and leads a morally impeccable life. If that were the case, churches would need to fire their elders—all of them. Rather, a man who is above reproach displays an exemplary degree of Christlikeness, free from conspicuous sin. Being "above reproach" is akin to being "respectable" (1 Tim. 3:2), "righteous," and "holy" (Titus 1:8).

In his book on elder qualifications, Thabiti Anyabwile puts it well: "Being above reproach means that an elder is to be the kind of man whom no one suspects of wrong-doing or immorality. People would be shocked to hear this kind of man charged with such acts."[1]

Nominating men who are above reproach to be elders stokes the congregation's trust in its leaders. Further, church leaders who are above reproach safeguard the church's witness to the community, for as Paul said, "He must have a good reputation among outsiders, so that he does not fall into disgrace and the Devil's trap" (1 Tim. 3:7).

Self-controlled. According to Paul's profiles, elders must be self-controlled, sober-minded, temperate, and disciplined. Self-control is a fruit of the Holy Spirit (Gal. 5:23) and a mark of the Christian life. In short, a Spirit-filled man is a self-controlled man.

Interestingly, in both lists, Paul warned against a particular manifestation of lack of self-control: addiction to wine. Drunkenness destroys lives and sucks people into further sin. I know a man who gave up drinking when he became an elder. He wanted to be above reproach when it came to drinking and a model for church members who battled alcoholism.

While Scripture does not require elders to abstain from alcohol, they must possess the capacity for self-denial that this brother displayed.

Do you conceal a secret addiction to alcohol, drugs, pornography, or gambling? Do you lose control with anger, spending, swearing, or gossiping? Do you need to postpone eldership for a season in order to devote yourself to crucifying some habitual sin and cultivating self-control?

Gentle. There is a famous Swahili proverb that says, "When the elephants fight, the grass is trampled." Likewise, when a church's shepherds are combative and aggressive, the sheep get hurt. That's why Paul described the qualified elder as "not a bully but gentle, not quarrelsome" (1 Tim. 3:3) and "not arrogant, not hot tempered" (Titus 1:7). Egotistical, domineering, argumentative, pushy, gruff, hotheaded, explosive overseers crush church members.

Instead, elders must be gentle giants. Gentleness does not mean weakness or cowardice. Gentle elders exercise their authority with the tenderness of a shepherd and the sensitivity of a loving father. I once watched a television program in which a tortoise crawled up next to an elephant that was drinking at a watering hole. The elephant looked down and gingerly moved the tortoise to the side with its toe so that it wouldn't crush the reptile accidentally. I was amazed to see that massive creature take such care. People are similarly amazed when they experience gentleness from a church leader.

Are you gentle or heavy-handed? Are you a peacemaker or a fire-starter? Do you listen well or talk over others to express your opinions? It is difficult to gauge these things in yourself.

Be brave and ask a few insightful church members to give you candid assessments.

Not greedy. Elders must not be "greedy for money." Peter said that elders must serve "not for the money but eagerly" (1 Pet. 5:2). These words offer a stinging rebuke to pastors who use their ministries to get rich and live large. Beware of shepherds who fleece the sheep.

Greed isn't a problem just for paid pastors. Lay elders who live to make money have difficulty investing time and energy into caring for the congregation. Sometimes greedy lay elders manipulate churches with their donations. They may control church budgets and steer funds toward pet ministries. They assess the church's health and success by the monthly treasurer's report. When money-loving men lead a church, spending toward the poor, church planting, and global evangelism dries up. Why invest heavily in causes that don't directly enrich the greedy elder's little fiefdom?

How do you relate to money? Do you love it and live to amass it? Or do you delight to give to the local church, the spread of the gospel, and the needs of others? Do you give a tithe or a token, a sacrifice or a symbol? Does your giving come with strings attached? Examine yourself carefully, "for the love of money is a root of all kinds of evil" (1 Tim. 6:10).

Before we move on, stop for a moment and think about Jesus. When the religious leaders accused him of being in league with the Devil, the charges didn't stick because he was *above reproach.* When the sword-brandishing Peter offered him an opportunity to avoid his captors, he remained *self-controlled,* determined to fulfill what he and the Father had planned at the cross. When dealing with the weak, hurting, and sick, he was *gentle*. When the Devil offered him the kingdoms of the world, he was not *greedy*. In all of these moments, Jesus was acting as God's perfect shepherd of the sheep, as well as marking out a pattern for elders in churches today.

3. You Can Teach the Bible

Paul said an overseer must be "an able teacher" (1 Tim. 3:2). Teaching the Bible is central to the elder's shepherding work. We will explore teaching more in chapter 3. But for now, simply reflect: "Have I instructed others from God's Word with notable effect?"

Over the years, our church's elders have discussed potential elder candidates. At times, someone has suggested a man who has been a believer and faithful church member for years. We talk about the man's godly character and his happy marriage. We list ministries and committees on which he has served, and realize this man has volunteered hundreds of hours. The more we talk, the more obvious it seems the man should be an elder.

Then someone asks, "Can he teach the Bible?"

Certainly the man in question has taught us by his godly example. But that's not what Paul meant when he required an elder to be able to teach. He meant fruitful verbal communication of the gospel and biblical doctrine. An elder must hold "to the faithful message as taught, so that he will be able both to encourage with sound teaching and to refute those who contradict it" (Titus 1:9).

In some cases, we realize the brother has never taught,

even in a small setting such as a home group. So we put the elder nomination on hold and explore the issue with the man in a follow-up conversation.

Elders shepherd the flock like Jesus. Just as Jesus proclaimed God's Word with authority, so potential elders must be known for teaching the Bible well.

4. You Lead Your Family Well

American society paints a bright line between public and private, work and home. We evaluate a business leader on his or her ability to increase profits and meet company goals, not on the quality of his or her personal life. The leader's home world—children, marriage, sex life—is no one else's business.

But in the family of God, an elder's home life matters immensely. In fact, marriage and parenting act as a proving ground for elder fitness. Consider three ways in which a man's family leadership qualifies him for church leadership. An elder must be:

A one-woman man. Most English Bibles translate Paul's words as "the husband of one wife" (1 Tim 3:2; Titus 1:6), but some render them as "a one-woman man." It's difficult to know precisely how to interpret this phrase.[2] But at the very least, it conveys the idea of a faithful husband who honors the sacred covenant of marriage.

Have you been sexually faithful to your wife? Do you frequent pornographic websites? Have you ever been divorced? How are things between you and your spouse right now? No one has a fairy-tale, friction-free marriage. But if your marriage is limping (or worse) or if you've had a marriage failure in the past, you should talk with a few wise elders and pastors before seeking eldership. How you handle your bride matters very much if you would care for Christ's bride.

Does the requirement that an elder be "a one-woman man" disqualify unmarried brothers from eldership? Given Paul's clear teaching elsewhere on the ministry advantages of singleness and his own example of being an unmarried apostle (1 Cor. 7:7, 25–38), it seems singleness itself should not bar a man from the office of overseer. Still, if you are unmarried, ask yourself: "Am I maintaining sexual purity? Am I above reproach in my dating relationships?"

An effective father: Management skill *does* matter for elders. Overseers should possess leadership ability, as implied in the title "overseer." However, we typically associate "management" with employees and policies, financials and strategic plans. Paul had in mind a different management venue: children and the home.

An elder is "one who manages his own household competently, having his children under control with all dignity. (If anyone does not know how to manage his own household, how will he take care of God's church?)" (1 Tim. 3:4–5).

Can you see similarities between being a dad and being an elder? In both cases, a man takes on a leadership role. In both, he bears the primary responsibility to help those under his care grow up and live together in harmony. Both parenting and eldering are about guiding people toward maturity within a community context. Learn to shepherd God's family by shepherding yours first.

Are your children well-behaved or out of control? Are you

instructing your children at home about God's Word and the gospel? Or are your children exasperated by either your excessive harshness or deficient engagement (Eph. 6:4)? Is the atmosphere of your home predominantly nurturing and orderly or toxic and chaotic?

Does this text exclude childless brothers from eldership? No, not on principle. However, if a married man refuses to have children in order to enjoy a certain lifestyle without kids getting in the way, we should be concerned. Has a love for the world kept him from obeying that basic marital command, "Be fruitful and multiply" (Gen. 1:28, ESV)? But if a man is childless for reasons beyond his control, he should demonstrate fruitful disciple-making somewhere in his life. Here's the principle: nominate men as shepherds who are *already* engaged in effective shepherding.

Hospitable. Paul twice commanded that overseers be "hospitable" (1 Tim. 3:2; Titus 1:8).

Hospitality can reveal kindness, compassion, and care for the needy, lost, and lonely, all qualities befitting an elder. But hospitality does something else: it allows others to see your family in action.

What do others see when they come over for dinner at your place? They don't see a flawless family, of course. But do your guests detect warmth and mutual respect in the tones and nonverbal signals between you and your wife? Between you and your kids? Do they see children obeying you, and you responding appropriately when your kids disobey? If your house were a church, would your dinner guests want to come back for another visit?

5. You Are Male

It should be obvious by now, but let me say it plainly: God has called men, and only men, to be church elders.[3] Consider a few observations:

- As we have seen, Paul said twice, in different contexts, that an overseer must be a one-woman *man*.
- Immediately before discussing overseers, Paul said, "I do not allow a woman to teach or to have authority over a man" (1 Tim. 2:12). Given the immediate context, this verse, at the very least, must apply to the role of overseer, which is fundamentally defined by both teaching and exercising authority.
- Paul linked leading a church to leading a family. Just as God has called men to lead in marriage and parenting (Eph. 5:22–6:4), so he calls men to lead in the church family.

Does this mean that women can never teach or shepherd, confront sin or model godliness? Of course not. You can probably think of godly women whom God has used to shepherd and shape you, as can I. But the eldership is more than a gifting or a ministry. *Elder* describes a specific office, a divinely appointed role, a distinct position within the organizational structure of a local church, just as *father* is a distinct, divinely appointed position in the family. And as with the role of father, so God has sovereignly summoned qualified *men* to the role of elder.

6. You Are an Established Believer

Paul cautioned against new Christians serving as elders: "He must not be a new convert, or he might become conceited and fall into the condemnation of the Devil" (1 Tim. 3:6).

Sometimes newly saved Christians amaze us by their spiritual enthusiasm, rapid transformation, and fearless evangelism. But be slow to put that energetic new Christian into eldership quickly. He has much growing and testing ahead. The term *elder* implies wisdom and experience, things a new believer lacks.

If you are a recent convert, focus on sinking your roots more deeply into Christ. Watch out for spiritual pride. In fact, let's walk it back a step: be sure you are truly converted. Don't assume! Have you repented of your sins and put your faith in Jesus to pardon you? Do you believe that only Jesus's death and resurrection can rescue you from hell and reconcile you to God? Are you born again? Nothing ruins churches like installing unconverted pastors and elders. How can someone serve as Jesus's under-shepherd and reflect Jesus's character if he isn't even a Christian?

Our church elects elders at an annual meeting. At that meeting, we ask elder nominees to tell the story of how they came to repent and believe in Jesus. The nominees are often men whom we have known for years and who have served as elders before. But the church wants to hear these men once again confess faith in Jesus. I'm not sure when our church started this practice, but I hope we never stop.

IS THAT YOU?

I want you to do something right now. Before turning to the next chapter, I want you to read 1 Timothy 3:1–7. Read it out loud. I'm totally serious. Go somewhere private if necessary, and read these verses aloud:

This saying is trustworthy: "If anyone aspires to be an overseer, he desires a noble work." An overseer, therefore, must be above reproach, the husband of one wife, self-controlled, sensible, respectable, hospitable, an able teacher, not addicted to wine, not a bully but gentle, not quarrelsome, not greedy—one who manages his own household competently, having his children under control with all dignity. (If anyone does not know how to manage his own household, how will he take care of God's church?) He must not be a new convert, or he might become conceited and fall into the condemnation of the Devil. Furthermore, he must have a good reputation among outsiders, so that he does not fall into disgrace and the Devil's trap.

That's what a man asked me to do when I was being examined for ordination to pastoral ministry. So I opened my Bible and read 1 Timothy 3:1–7 aloud to the man and the others in the room. When I finished, the man said to me: "Thank you for reading that. I have only one question. Is that you?" Then he sat down.

We must resemble Jesus if we want to lead his churches, and Jesus embodies all of these characteristics. The sheep should detect strong traces of the Chief Shepherd in the lives and character of would-be under-shepherds. So may I ask, based on the description of an elder you just read, "Is that you?"

2

SMELL LIKE SHEEP

"So this church is like your business, and you're in sales, and God is the product," the newcomer said as we stood in the foyer after the church service. (I wish I kept a journal of all the strange post-sermon conversations I've had at the back of the church!)

"No, not really," I replied.

The man was simply trying to make sense of the church based on his experiences. He apparently knew business and sales, so he tried to interpret the church from what he knew.

Unfortunately, church newbies aren't the only ones who make this mistake. Pastors, elders, and members often misinterpret the church through business and organizational lenses.

Granted, churches have business aspects. Churches often use financial officers and budgets, employees and personnel policies, facilities and insurance, workflow diagrams and goals, bylaws and committees. These are parts of a congregation's life and need to be managed well for God's glory. A local church is an organized organism.

The problem arises when these businesslike elements become part of a comprehensive business model for the congregation that ignores biblical teaching. It might look something like this:

- Pastor = president/CEO
- Staff = vice presidents
- Members = shareholders/loyal customers
- Visitors = potential customers

And the elders' role?

- Elders = board of trustees

In this model, the elders' job description is similar to that for the members of a board of trustees. They hire the pastor(s) to do and lead the work of ministry. The elders then gather at board meetings to assess the ministry, watch the finances, and set the policies. The pastors bring forward new initiatives and the elders approve or reject them. Pastors minister and elders direct.

But this eldership model fails to incorporate a key biblical truth: the elders are pastors too.

ELDER = PASTOR

Somehow, somewhere along the way, we have differentiated pastors from elders, the paid ministry pros from the unpaid trustees. But the New Testament makes no such distinction.

What is a pastor anyway? The Greek word *poimen*, which we translate as "pastor," means "shepherd." *Poimen* can refer to a literal shepherd, like the ones out in the fields in Luke's Christmas story. Far more often, however, *poimen* refers to

Jesus, our Good Shepherd. There's also a related verb, *poimaino,* which means "to shepherd" or "to tend a flock." So a pastor is a shepherd, and pastoring means caring for a flock. Not surprisingly, our English word *pastor* comes from the Latin word *pastor*, which means . . . shepherd!

This part is critical: the New Testament applies these noun and verb forms of "shepherd," as well as broader shepherding imagery, to describe *elders and their work*. Look at the following verses, in which I have italicized the places where *poimaino* and *poimen* are translated into English.

Paul warns the elders of the church in Ephesus:

> Be on guard for yourselves and for all the flock that the Holy Spirit has appointed you to as overseers, *to shepherd* the church of God, which He purchased with His own blood. (Acts 20:28)

Similarly, Peter writes:

> I exhort the elders among you: *Shepherd* God's flock among you, not overseeing out of compulsion but freely, according to God's will; not for the money but eagerly; not lording it over those entrusted to you, but being examples to the flock. And when the chief *Shepherd* appears, you will receive the unfading crown of glory. (1 Pet. 5:1–4)

Peter's words sound reminiscent of what Jesus said to him after the resurrection: "Feed My lambs" and "*Shepherd* My sheep" (John 21:15, 16).

And what about the officers that Jesus gave as gifts to his church? Paul lists apostles, prophets, evangelists, and then "*pastors* and teachers" (Eph. 4:11). The Greek grammar makes clear that "pastor" and "teacher" go together to describe one office or role. So the pastors, or shepherds, of the church are also its teachers. And as we've already seen, teaching is at the heart of the office of elder.

THE REAL DEAL

A friend of mine who served as a lay elder told me, "One of the hardest things about being an elder was believing I was a *real* pastor." But the Bible couldn't be clearer. If you are an elder in your church, you are a genuine pastor, just as much as, well, the paid pastor.

Maybe you still have doubts. Aren't there differences between the "special" guys who serve as paid pastors for their careers and the "regular" guys who work other jobs but volunteer as elders? Yes, there are differences. For example, paid pastors often have more formal theological education, more time during the week to serve, and therefore more experience in pastoring, church ministry, and teaching. It's also possible—though not necessarily the case—that paid pastors have stronger giftings in pastoral care or preaching, which is why churches hire them to minister on a full-time basis.

But just because a paid pastor may have more availability, education, or gifting, it doesn't follow logically (or biblically) that a lay elder is any less a real pastor. Volunteer firefighters face the same flames as the paid firefighters, and volunteer elders confront the same challenges of shepherding as the staff pastors. Lay elders may honor vocational pastors as "firsts among equals,"[1] but the lay elders are still equals.

A REVOLUTIONARY MODEL

In light of all this, if we had to summarize an elder's job description, we might simply say, "Shepherd the flock." If you remember only one thing from this book, then, let it be that elders are pastors/shepherds, and their core job is to tend the church's members like shepherds tend their sheep. To be more precise, elders are under-shepherds who serve the Good Shepherd by leading *his* sheep.

So what, then, does "shepherding" entail? What does it look like in action? The following chapters will examine the various dimensions of shepherding. We will talk about such things as teaching, leading, and praying.

But before we look at the "how-to's" of the shepherding task, we need to explore two overarching implications of the elder-as-shepherd model. Really grasping that elders are pastors, not just trustees for non-profit organizations, could revolutionize our elder ministry in at least two major ways.

SMELL LIKE SHEEP

The first revolutionary implication of an elder-as-shepherd model is that elders are to engage in *relationships with church members.*

Stop for a moment and envision a literal shepherd. Perhaps you have seen one at work in the countryside, whether in person or in a movie. Maybe you have never seen one but have read enough about shepherds in the Bible that you can paint a mental picture. What do you see? Do you envision an Irish farmer leading his flock across a lush green pasture? Perhaps you imagine a robed Bedouin with a crook shooing a lamb into a makeshift stone pen. Or maybe you recite Psalm 23 and visualize a shepherd making his sheep lie down in green pastures and drink at quiet waters.

Whatever we each imagine, there is probably at least one common feature to our mental screenshots. In all of them, the shepherd is *among* the sheep. He's not off somewhere else. He is walking in the midst of the animals, touching them and speaking to them. He knows them because he lives with them. As a result, he even smells like sheep.

Maybe, instead of visualizing literal shepherds, simply think of Jesus. In the Gospels, we find Jesus constantly *among* the people. Except for periods of private prayer, it seems Jesus spent all his time with his disciples, as well as with the crowds. He touched, taught, and trained people wherever he went. The Good Shepherd not only laid down his life for the sheep, but he also spent his life with them.

Just as literal shepherds live among their flocks and know their sheep, and just as Jesus immersed himself in relationships with his disciples, so elders share their lives with church members. They see people as their ministry. The following chapters cover various components of eldership, but all of them assume that elders live in close relational proximity to their brothers and sisters.

Let's take one example for now: hospitality. As we saw in the last chapter, both of Paul's overseer qualification lists require that a man desiring the role must be hospitable (1 Tim. 3:2; Titus 1:8). Why this emphasis on hospitality? Hospitality not only reveals a generous heart and a servant's attitude, but it also shows that the aspiring overseer wants to be with people and looks for ways to welcome people into his life. A hospitable man likely wants to be among the people if the church appoints him as an elder.

By contrast, overseers operating in an elder-as-trustee model need not be among the people. They can attend monthly meetings, participate in board debates, cast votes, and then go home with a sense of having fulfilled their duties. When this model dominates, elders don't have to get their hands dirty wrestling with what to say to a member discouraged by fourteen months of unemployment, to a brother battling temptations to relapse into shooting heroin, or to a sister who has gotten into a serious dating relationship with an unbelieving man and doesn't see any problem with it. They think, "Didn't we hire a pastor to deal with those messes?"

You may indeed have called a pastor with those responsibilities in mind. But if you're a lay elder, it's time to wade into the flock alongside the paid staff and do some hands-on, heartfelt pastoring yourself.

YOU'VE GOT THE WRONG GUY FOR THE JOB!

Does this kind of people-work sound intimidating?

Maybe you're thinking: "I'm not good with people. I'm better with numbers or computers or power tools. I'm an introvert. I took a personality test that proved it. To be honest, I'm fairly quirky."

You don't have to be an extrovert or the life of the party to connect with your members. You just need to love them. Take the initiative to strike up a conversation before a church service with that quiet, elderly widow, invite a struggling couple over for dinner, or start a Bible study and invite some less connected members. People know real love and concern when they see it, even if it comes in a shy or slightly awkward package. Love leaps over all kinds of obstacles.

Maybe you have another hesitation when it comes to a pastoral ministry among the members. Maybe you fear getting in over your head with people's problems and making things worse by inept attempts to help. You don't have a counseling degree or seminary training. Who are you to start playing pastor?

To be clear, I'm not suggesting that anyone who simply desires to be an elder is therefore qualified. I am saying that qualified men should not unnecessarily disqualify themselves because of a fear that they can't solve people's life struggles.

Here are a few quick thoughts on caring for people who are facing big problems:

- God established elders in his Word and he knows what he's doing.
- Jesus can work through you.
- Shepherding isn't primarily about solving people's problems (more on this below).
- You likely have more biblical wisdom to share than you think.
- You can always ask for help, from Jesus and others.

SLOWLY MAKING THE TRANSITION

Some thirty years ago, the Baptist church where I serve called a Presbyterian to be the senior pastor. He was a gifted expositor who drew large crowds and affected many lives with the gospel. But he did something else that has continued to bless our church years after his departure: he led our congregation to adopt an elder model of governance.

By the time I came to the church, it had had elders in place for more than a decade. But as we studied biblical eldership more seriously, it became apparent that we elders were out of balance. We spent the majority of our energy acting like trustees of the organization and far less pastoring the people. So we began slowly shifting more attention to shepherding. We still have our monthly meetings and still do trustee kinds of things. Again, that is a component of the elder role and of church life. But we have also been attempting to invest more time with the church members.

For instance, more than a year ago, we divided our expanding church membership list among the elders and then set the goal of reaching out to each member on our list at least once during the year. It was a small step, almost remedial. But even that small step bore immediate fruit. Members not only responded with appreciation, they also became more willing to open up their lives to the elders. The elders found this kind of pastoral ministry challenging but also highly rewarding. In addition, I was relieved to have a broader team to help carry the load of a growing congregation.

We still have a long way to go. But our elders are smelling more and more like sheep.

WHAT'S THE GOAL?

Let's recap: elders are pastors, or "shepherds." The shepherding metaphor carries significant implications for elder ministry. First, it suggests that elder work takes place primarily in relationships with church members. Eldering is more about people than programs.

But the shepherding imagery not only tells us the *where* of an elder's job—namely, in relationships—it also tells us the *why*. Why should elders hang out and share life with members? What are they trying to accomplish? Is the goal merely to give the church a more friendly, family vibe?

Here's a second revolutionary implication of the shepherding model: elders minister with the goal of *growing church members in Christian maturity*.

Visualize your shepherd again. Imagine him doing his daily, among-the-sheep tasks: feeding the flock, leading them across a valley, protecting them from wild animals, tending an infected leg, or tracking down a stray ewe. Why does the shepherd do these things? What is the purpose or goal? It is mature sheep. The shepherd toils day after day in order to produce healthy, full-grown sheep that reproduce.

Don't elders have a similar goal? Elders work hard in relationships with church members in order to help them grow up in Jesus. Overseers teach, pray, and serve so that their brothers and sisters might know Jesus more intimately, obey him more faithfully, and reflect his character more clearly, both individually and as a church family. Furthermore, healthy, mature believers reproduce themselves spiritually as they share the gospel with others and help others grow in Christ.

Paul explicitly names maturity as the goal of pastoral ministry:

And He [Jesus] personally gave some to be apostles, some prophets, some evangelists, some pastors and teachers, for the training of the saints in the work of ministry, to build up the body of Christ, until we all reach unity in the faith and in the knowledge of God's Son, growing into a mature man with a stature measured by Christ's fullness. (Eph. 4:11–13)

When elders fulfill their duties well, believers are "no longer . . . little children," but instead "grow in every way into Him who is the head—Christ" (vv. 14–15). Elders should strive to say with Paul, "We proclaim Him, warning and teaching everyone with all wisdom, so that we may present everyone mature in Christ" (Col. 1:28).

MANAGING THE MACHINE

Contrast this shepherding mentality again with the elder-as-trustee model. When elders see themselves primarily as members of a board of trustees, they perceive their purpose as managing the organizational elements of the church. "Success" likely means keeping balance sheets in the black, maintaining the facilities, and sponsoring high-quality, well-attended programs and events. Trustee elders are tempted to emphasize managing the machine over maturing the members.

We have already noted that the organizational infrastructure of a church—its budgets, processes, programs, facilities, personnel—*does* matter. Effective administration is a ministry and a spiritual gifting in itself that serves the whole body and liberates elders to shepherd. A little thought to organization empowered Moses in the Old Testament and the apostles in the New Testament to fulfill their callings, and God's people were blessed as a result (Ex. 18:13–27; Acts 6:1–7). And even as relational shepherds, the elders bear an overall responsibility to superintend the church's organizational infrastructure.

But here's the key: the organization must always serve the organism. Programs and processes at best provide tools for accomplishing the mission of maturing one another in Christ.

My experience has been that elders easily gravitate toward the machine rather than the members, the trellis rather than the vine,[2] giving more conversation and effort to fine-tuning logistics rather than laboring over the development of people. I'm not completely sure why this is. Maybe it's because programs and policies are manageable things that can be planned and accomplished, whereas the work of helping people grow in Christ is messy, non-linear, and slow. In fact, shepherding people is a task that we never fully accomplish in this life and cannot control.

Elders must resist the drift toward being mere organizational managers and instead keep the congregational compass pointed toward maturity in Jesus. To assist in this, at your next elder meeting, put a question or two like these on the agenda for discussion:

- In what ways does our congregation most reflect Jesus? In what ways do we not reflect him?
- Are there unresolved conflicts in the church in which we elders could attempt to facilitate reconciliation?
- Do we know of any members who have strayed into blatant sin or simply wandered from regular fellowship in the church? Who is talking to them?

- What biblical books or theological doctrines do our members need to study in the coming year? Why?
- Do our members know how to evangelize and disciple others? Are they doing it?
- Are we a praying church?

PASSING THE MANTLE

When Jesus departed for heaven, he gave these final instructions to his followers:

> Go, therefore, and make disciples of all nations, baptizing them in the name of the Father and of the Son and of the Holy Spirit, teaching them to observe everything I have commanded you. (Matt. 28:19–20)

Jesus told his disciples to do what he had been doing with them for the previous few years. He had gathered his disciples, marked them off, and caused them to grow by teaching them his commands. The Good Shepherd not only laid down his life for those sheep, but also lived among them and transformed them. Jesus made disciples: people who loved him, obeyed him, and told others about him.

Now Jesus was sending those disciples to make disciples. The apostles would take up Jesus's shepherding mantle and call more Christ followers, gather them into churches, and help them to grow up through teaching.

After the apostles established those local congregations of disciples, they, too, passed the mantle of relational, maturity-minded pastoring. To whom did they pass it?

To church elders!

3

SERVE UP THE WORD

I think the elders were in shock.

We had gathered for our annual elder retreat to discuss goals for the upcoming year, as well as to revisit the biblical job description for overseers. When the topic of teaching came up, I issued a challenge: "Sometime this year, I want two elders to preach during Sunday morning services."

Although lay elders preach in some congregations, our church had always left Sunday morning sermons to paid pastors. Lay preaching was only for dire emergencies. So it wasn't surprising that the elders responded to my challenge with wide-eyed stares and a few nervous chuckles.

But I wasn't trying to be outrageous. I only wanted to nudge them toward their biblical calling to teach the Word. If elders shepherd Jesus's sheep, then their most basic task is to feed the souls of church members from the Scriptures. Without food, sheep weaken and die, and without regular nourishment through biblical teaching, Christians starve spiritually.

Perhaps more than any other task, teaching sets elders apart in a local church. We saw in chapter 1 that qualified elders must be able to teach (1 Tim. 3:2). It's worth noticing that Paul's qualification lists in 1 Timothy 3 for elders and deacons are rather similar, except for one glaring difference: elders must be apt to teach the Word, whereas deacons have no such requirement. Both elders and deacons need Christlike character, but only elders must demonstrate skill in explaining and applying the Bible.

In chapter 2, we meditated on the truth that elders are pastors, or shepherds. When Paul lists various offices gifted to the church by Jesus, he fuses pastoring with teaching: "And He personally gave some to be apostles, some prophets, some evangelists, some pastors and teachers" (Eph. 4:11).

Notice two things. First, all these officeholders communicate God's Word. The apostles are eyewitnesses who proclaim and inscripturate Jesus's words and deeds. Prophets deliver direct words from the Lord. Evangelists herald the gospel. Likewise, pastors teach local churches. That leads to the second observation: the words *pastor* and *teacher* in verse 11 go together. In the Greek, one definite article governs both nouns, signaling that the two nouns modify one another. So "pastors and teachers" does not refer to two roles but to one, that of a "pastor-teacher."

GOD RULES BY HIS WORD

The fact that God requires elders to teach his people shouldn't surprise us. God rules his people by his Word, so the leaders of God's people have always been entrusted with communicating God's Word.

God spoke his promises to Abraham, Isaac, and Jacob, who in turn led their clans to trust those promises and obey God.

God gave the words of the covenant to Moses, who taught them to Israel (Deut. 4:1). Moses commanded the dads in Israel to shepherd their children by teaching them the Law (Deut. 4:9; 6:4–25), a command repeated to believing dads in the church (Eph. 6:4). The priests in Israel not only offered sacrifices, but also taught the people God's decrees (Lev. 10:10–11; 2 Chron. 15:3; 17:7–9). God guided and corrected his people by sending prophets who announced, "Thus says the Lord." Even the king of Israel was expected to be a serious student of God's Law (Deut. 17:18–20).

Then there was Jesus. Our Good Shepherd was first and foremost a mighty preacher. When he saw the crowds, he "had compassion on them, because they were like sheep without a shepherd." And what did he do to meet their need for a shepherd? "He began to teach them many things" (Mark 6:34). The four Gospels are replete with Jesus's parables, interpretations, exhortations, and dialogues. Jesus is the Word incarnate (John 1:1, 14), who fulfilled all the words of the Old Testament (Matt. 5:17; Luke 24:25–27, 44–47) and poured forth God's Word throughout his public ministry.

After his resurrection, Jesus passed on his teaching and proclamation ministry to the apostles (Matt. 28:19–20). Just as Jesus's teaching fills the Gospels, so the apostles' teaching fills Acts and the Epistles. And as the apostles made disciples through their preaching and gathered those disciples into churches, they appointed elders for each church and entrusted them with the apostolic doctrine (Acts 14:23).

Take a moment to marvel at this. Jesus is alive. He reigns in heaven and he rules over your church. And he exerts that kingly authority in your church through the Scriptures. Jesus's subjects obey him today by obeying those Scriptures. So if you are an elder, when you teach the Word faithfully, Jesus is sovereignly ministering to his subjects through your teaching.

PARTICIPATE IN THE TEACHING

What does this mean, practically speaking, for elders? What are the implications for an elder's job description? I believe there are two. The first should be obvious: elders must *participate* in the teaching ministry of the church. If you are an elder, you need to get busy expounding the Bible.

Yet elders often shy away from teaching. Even qualified elders who are able to teach the Word pull back from opportunities to instruct. It happens for a number of reasons, with the most common being a sense of inadequacy. Lay elders compare their own natural ability, teaching experience, and theological training to that of their paid pastor(s), and sometimes discouragement ensues. They think, "Why would church members want to hear from an amateur like me when we have pros on staff?" Furthermore, lay overseers often work long hours outside the church and so lack extended time for lesson preparation. Who wants to serve the sheep a half-baked meal?

But if you're an elder, you *are* a teacher. So don't let these fears and frustrations keep you from teaching. Instead, be encouraged and execute your calling to the best of your ability and resources.

Be encouraged by the fact that teaching takes place in a wide variety of venues. It isn't confined to the Sunday morning sermon. Elders can feed the flock in large gatherings or intimate settings. You can open the Bible for a Sunday school class, a home group, a Vacation Bible School for kids, or a one-to-one mentoring relationship. Look for teaching needs anywhere in the church and step in to help.

Our congregation includes a small group of people from Cambodia. Between 1981 and 1982, some of our members sponsored them to come to the United States during the Cambodian refugee crisis. Many of these refugees have become believers and church members. They have a Sunday school class conducted in Khmer, the language of Cambodia. I have been touched over the years watching elders teach that class through an interpreter. The elders saw the need and crossed the cultural and language barriers to feed the flock.

Be encouraged as well by the fact that the gifting to teach comes in a variety of strengths and packages. If you lack the ability to hold a large congregation in rapt attention for forty-five minutes, that doesn't mean you should abdicate your call to teach. Stop the fruitless comparisons and figure out how to use the gifts, life experiences, and personality God has given you.

Michael, a member of my church, had a heart for men who had been broken by years of enslavement to sinful addictions, primarily because Jesus had rescued him from the guilt and power of addiction. So he started an "addictions" Bible study. That's what it was: a Bible study. Michael didn't use a recovery program curriculum. He just taught the Bible. But his life experience and compassion enabled him to connect with men battling addiction in a different way than I do in my regular Sunday preaching. Michael wasn't even an elder, but his example shows how God uses our varied life experiences for teaching his Word.

Finally, be encouraged that Bible teachers can improve. Every teacher should follow Paul's instructions to Timothy:

> Until I come, give your attention to public reading, exhortation and teaching. Do not neglect the gift that is in you; it was given to you through prophecy, with the laying on of hands by the council of elders. Practice these things; be committed to them, so that your progress may be evident to all. (1 Tim. 4:13–15)

God calls his teachers to show progress, not perfection. Don't compare yourself to other teachers; instead, compare your teaching to what it was last year or five years ago and look for improvement. We improve when we "practice these things" (that is, "public reading, exhortation and teaching") and when we are "committed to them."

So take opportunities to teach. Push yourself. If you have theologically trained men in your church, ask them for book recommendations to shore up weak spots in your knowledge. And ask other teachers and elders to listen to your lessons and give feedback.

If your regular preaching pastor asks whether you want to bring the sermon on a Sunday morning, take a risk and say, "Yes!"

PROTECT THE TEACHING

There is a second dimension to an elder's teaching labors. An overseer not only participates in teaching, he also must protect the church from false teaching. He must play both doctrinal offense and defense, "holding to the faithful message as taught, so that he will be able both to encourage with sound teaching and to refute those who contradict it" (Titus 1:9).

Predators hunt sheep. Just as shepherds ward off lions and wolves, so elders must ward off false teachers. Paul warned the elders in Ephesus:

> I know that after my departure savage wolves will come in among you, not sparing the flock. And men will rise up from your own number with deviant doctrines to lure the disciples into following them. Therefore be on the alert, remembering that night and day for three years I did not stop warning each one of you with tears. (Acts 20:29–31)

Paul must have had a particular concern for false teaching in Ephesus, because in his letter to the church he again stressed the importance of the pastoral teaching ministry so that believers might grow up and withstand the pressures and allurements of false doctrine. When sound teaching does its work, "then we will no longer be little children, tossed by the waves and blown around by every wind of teaching, by human cunning with cleverness in the techniques of deceit" (Eph. 4:14).

Strategies for Keeping Watch

Opposing false teaching demands vigilance. Elders need to be alert for people or ideas that would distort the gospel or twist the Bible. Here are three strategies for keeping watch over your flock:

Know Your Context

Start by studying your spiritual surroundings. Familiarize yourself with the particular beliefs, philosophies, and religions that are active in your community. Do your people come into regular contact with another major religion? Does some cult have a strong presence in your city? Be aware of these groups' major teachings, especially where they contradict the gospel and biblical truth.

What about the "isms"? Do attitudes of secularism, individualism, rationalism, or relativism mold people's thinking where you live? Local people coming to your church will import these alternative beliefs and operate in the church on the basis of these "isms" without even realizing it. Be sure to call out these worldviews in your teaching and conversations.

Be particularly aware of gospel distortions active among churches around you, or even in your own church. These might be anything from the prosperity gospel to open theism to legalism to theological liberalism. Are local charismatic personalities winning followers to gospel-lite or gospel-counterfeit teachings? All these teachings can harm your sheep.

Monitor Your Membership Process

While you scan the horizon of your local landscape, don't forget to watch the front gate of the sheep pen. Who is joining your church? Do new members know what your church teaches? Do they agree with it? Are you sure?

An intentional membership process goes a long way toward guarding your church from false teaching. Prospective

members should hear what your church believes before joining. My elders and I have learned over the years that some of
our church's theological distinctives cause more heartburn
for people than others. These distinctives include believer's
baptism, Reformed theology, and male eldership. So we intentionally address these more controversial beliefs up front in
our membership class. If someone in the class forgoes membership and leaves the church because of those positions, we
have shown him or her a kindness in the long run.

You also need to learn what prospective members believe.
Consider conducting elder interviews with those seeking
church membership. Ask people directly whether they understand the church's doctrinal positions and agree with them.
Some churches even ask new members to sign the church's
doctrinal statement to affirm the congregation's theological
commitments.

It should go without saying, but let me say it anyway: never
allow non-members a regular teaching role in your fellowship.

Audit Your Ministries

Do you know what's being taught in your church? Use your
elder credentials to slip into a youth talk or sit in the back of a
women's event. Help out a few times in Sunday school. What
kind of spiritual nourishment are your people receiving? Is it
grade A gospel or theological rot? Listen to your congregational
music with a discerning ear. What messages do the lyrics teach
about God, the gospel, or salvation? Is your singing supporting
or subverting your doctrine?

Take the audit down to the grassroots level. Good shepherding happens when elders tune in to the people themselves. What are they reading? Do they follow certain preachers on the Internet? If members are excitedly passing a book around the church, you should probably give it a read.

If you find a Bible study leader, a Sunday school teacher, or a persuasive talker torpedoing sound doctrine, address him or her directly. Don't let the situation fester. It will not get better on its own. The apostles leveled their harshest indictments against false teachers (2 Peter 2; 2 John 7–11; Jude 5–11), and Jesus gave dire warnings to churches that accommodated them (Rev. 2:14–16, 20–23).

Recognizing the Real Thing

Perhaps the most important thing elders can do to guard against counterfeit teaching is to know genuine biblical truth. By "holding to the faithful message as taught," elders are able "to refute those who contradict it" (Titus 1:9). Heresies and half-truths are legion, but there's only one truth. The more you know your Bible, the more you can detect even the most subtle false teaching.

There was a church whose leaders felt the pastor had drifted from the gospel. The pastor was smart and more educated than the leaders, and he seemingly could prove his position from the Scriptures. But despite his superior learning and eloquence, the new teaching still didn't sit well with the church leaders. They didn't recognize it as the faithful message they had known, even if they couldn't win a debate against their minister or even precisely pinpoint where he had gone awry. They confronted the pastor, and he eventually left the church.

It doesn't take a seminary degree to protect the church's doctrine, but it does take courage and faith.

PERPETUATE THE TEACHING

This chapter has been a plea for elders to participate in and protect sound teaching. But perhaps you are already doing that. In fact, you may be a master teacher, able to untie the most complex theological knots and tie up the most agile false teachers. Nevertheless, there's still one major problem facing your teaching ministry: you are going to die.

When you die, you will, by God's grace, leave behind many well-taught Christians. But will you also leave behind skilled teachers to carry on the work? In other words, have you taken steps to train others? Part of teaching the church is training future pastor-teachers. As Paul told Timothy, "What you have heard from me in the presence of many witnesses, commit to faithful men who will be able to teach others also" (2 Tim. 2:2).

Have you noticed another man in the church who seems to show promise as a teacher or elder? Consider meeting with him regularly to read theology or do a Bible study. Or maybe take him on as a kind of apprentice in your home Bible study or in the Sunday school class you teach. Walk him through your process for developing a lesson, let him teach, and then give him feedback. Rinse and repeat.

BUCKLE UP

Kevin was one of the elders who accepted my challenge to preach a Sunday morning sermon. Shortly after agreeing to the assignment, he told me that he had a growing burden for reaching his town and wondered whether God had been calling him to help start a church there. Kevin teaches at a high school in the town and coaches track and soccer. He literally knows hundreds of people in his community. What an ideal person to help lead a church plant there! The idea that he could actually preach on a Sunday morning breathed new life into that dream.

Today, Kevin is doing a preaching-focused internship at our church. He's studying biblical exposition through an online course put out by the Simeon Trust, as well as taking regular opportunities to teach and receive feedback. I don't know what all the next steps will be or whether a church plant will come to fruition. That is all in God's hands. But I do see an elder leaning into his calling to teach, making progress, and daring to dream big for the gospel.

4

TRACK DOWN
THE STRAYS

It's an all-too-common phenomenon in churches. A church member stops showing up on Sunday mornings. A few weeks pass, and then a few months, before someone notices. It might happen more easily in larger churches, but it can happen in small churches, too.

People in my congregation refer to this phenomenon as "falling through the cracks." They say things like: "Have you seen Sally around church lately? I hope she didn't fall through the cracks." But is that how it happens? Is it really like falling through a crack? Such a description likens the church to a tree house far above the ground, with large gaps between the wooden planks of the floor. Occasionally a member fails to pay attention, steps into a gap, and disappears with a "whoosh." Do members really leave churches abruptly, accidentally, and without any opportunity for people to notice?

What if, instead of "falling through the cracks," we use a different image: "straying from the flock." That picture seems more fitting for at least two reasons. First, "straying" implies that a disconnected church member bears a personal responsibility to stay involved with the congregation. Sheep don't ordinarily leave a flock by inadvertently plummeting into a void. They wander away over time through a series of choices.

Second, the image of straying sheep also suggests that someone should keep watch over the flock and take action when a sheep begins to meander away. Yes, each member has a personal responsibility not to roam, but all church members have a duty to watch out for one another. However, one group in particular has an obligation to be on the lookout for straying sheep: the elders.

KEEPING WATCH

In chapter 3, we saw that elders watch to make sure that no "wolves" infiltrate their congregations with false teaching. But elders also keep watch for unwanted movement in the other direction: members straying away from the flock and from the Lord. This is part of basic shepherding work. Shepherds feed the sheep, guard them from predators, and keep track of them.

Remember when Jacob recounted his toil of watching Laban's flocks? Jacob lamented how he exhausted himself overseeing Laban's sheep and how he gave an account for each animal. In his complaint, we get a glimpse of vigilant, accountable shepherding:

> I've been with you these 20 years. Your ewes and female goats have not miscarried, and I have not eaten the rams from your flocks. I did not bring you any of the flock torn by wild beasts; I myself bore the loss. You demanded payment from me for what was stolen by day or by night. There I was—the heat consumed

me by day and the frost by night, and sleep fled from my eyes. (Gen. 31:38–40)

In contrast, Ezekiel prophesied against Israel's leaders by accusing them of negligent shepherding: "Woe to the shepherds of Israel, who have been feeding themselves! Shouldn't the shepherds feed their flock?" (Ezek. 34:2). And what was one of the ways they failed to shepherd? "You have not . . . brought back the strays, or sought the lost" (v. 4). As a result, "My flock went astray on all the mountains and every high hill. They were scattered over the whole face of the earth, and there was no one searching or seeking for them" (v. 6).

However, God announced that he himself would come looking for the lost sheep of his people:

> But this is what the Lord GOD says: See, I Myself will search for My flock and look for them. As a shepherd looks for his sheep on the day he is among his scattered flock, so I will look for My flock. (Ezek. 34:11–12)

So God came in Jesus, gathering lost sheep into a new flock. Jesus explained his ministry to tax collectors and sinners by comparing himself to a shepherd leaving ninety-nine "found" sheep in order to look for one that was lost (Luke 15:1–7). He called himself the good shepherd who not only laid down his life for the sheep, but who would also bring in the "other sheep," a reference to the Gentiles (John 10:14–16).

Once again, here is where church elders come into the picture. Elders serve as Jesus's under-shepherds, keeping watch over the flocks that have been saved and gathered by

Jesus and his gospel. Elders are aptly named "overseers." They "keep watch over your souls as those who will give an account" (Heb. 13:17). This, in part, is why leading your family well is an elder qualification (see chapter 1). Good parenting requires attentive oversight of children and family dynamics, and so does good pastoring.

ACCOUNTABLE FOR WHOM?

All this oversight talk raises a critical question: Who exactly are the elders supposed to watch? If elders are shepherds who must give an account like Jacob did, then for whom are they accountable before God? Certainly church elders are not spiritually liable for every Christian everywhere. So elders must be responsible only for watching over those who attend the church where they serve. Right?

Well, maybe. Or maybe not. Do elders shoulder a spiritual responsibility for someone who has attended the church once? Twice? How long and how regularly must a person come to Sunday worship before he "officially" is counted as part of the fold that the elders oversee? What if a person attends a church Bible study regularly, but not church services? And does it make a difference if a regular attendee is a believer or an unbeliever?

It seems that biblical shepherding requires some clear way of defining the flock. Elders need to be able to distinguish the people for whom they are accountable as shepherds and the people to whom they are to relate as fellow Christians. To put it another way, church eldership requires some concept of church membership.

ELDERSHIP AND MEMBERSHIP

Church membership does two vital things. First, it *identifies* people as disciples of Jesus. Church membership doesn't make people Christians, but it does outwardly mark them as Christians. Jesus gave authority to local churches to "bind" and "loose" (Matt. 18:18), to tag sheep as sheep through baptism into membership (28:18–20) and to remove the tag through excommunication (18:15–17). In seeking church membership, a person presents himself to the church and says, "I'm a disciple," and the church says, "Yes, we believe you are!" (or, in rare instances, "No, we don't believe you are!"). In excommunication, the church says, "You may be a true Christian, but your unrepentant sin gives us no reason to continue affirming that you are."

Second, church membership not only identifies people as Christians, it also *gathers* a group of identified believers into a specific congregation, where they commit themselves to one another. The apostles made disciples by preaching the gospel and then baptizing and congregating those disciples into local fellowships so that the Christians could be taught to obey the commands of Jesus. When the apostles congregated groups of disciples, they appointed elders to lead and teach each church. As Paul reminded his coworker Titus, "The reason I left you in Crete was to set right what was left undone and, as I directed you, to appoint elders in every town" (Titus 1:5).

Can you see how church membership makes the whole elder oversight project possible?

By identifying and marking disciples of Jesus, church membership enables a pastor-elder to know that these sheep are, in fact, sheep, to the best of the church's knowledge. And by gathering disciples into a congregation, church membership helps an elder know which specific sheep are the ones under his oversight. He will give an account to God for *them* (Heb. 13:17). This doesn't mean that an elder should be indifferent or calloused to a non-member attending a church worship service. But it does mean that that elder has a type of authority and accountability toward members that he doesn't have toward non-members.

Church membership also helps the whole congregation remember that they are accountable for one another. Elders should take a lead role in looking out for straying sheep, but they are not the only watchmen. Membership means mutual accountability and concern within the whole body.

Is your church getting serious about a more biblical approach to eldership or considering moving to an elder model? Be sure to work on church membership simultaneously.[1] Intentional church membership creates the context for effective eldership.

FIVE SPECIES OF STRAYING SHEEP

Assume for a moment that you are an elder who gets it. You understand that your calling includes keeping an eye out for wayward members. Also assume your church practices intentional church membership, so you actually know whom you are supposed to watch. What now? How do you go about keeping watch? What should you be looking for in particular?

Here are five common ways church members go astray. As you engage relationally with your local fellowship and hear of a member in one of these situations, take note: that brother or sister could already be straying.

Sinning Sheep

Let's start with an easy situation—not necessarily easy to address, but easy to recognize. If you discover that one of your church members is engaged in open sin, then you have a straying, sinning sheep in need of intervention.

Every church member struggles with sin, as does every elder. John writes, "If we say, 'We have no sin,' we are deceiving ourselves, and the truth is not in us" (1 John 1:8). Yet some sins are more public and obvious than others, and at times members seem to stop struggling and embrace disobedience. So when sin that is both apparent and unrepentant comes to an elder's attention, he needs to summon his courage, trust in the Lord, and humbly confront the member just as Jesus taught us to do (Matt. 18:15–17).

Sometimes the intervention works. I rejoice as I remember times I challenged a member entangled in sin, and, despite my trepidation, the Lord graciously brought the person to repentance. However, it doesn't always work out that way. I know of an elder who was so intent on contacting an elusive errant member that he parked outside the member's business during the lunch hour in hopes of finally confronting him. Unfortunately, that member evaded him and never repented or returned.

Wandering Sheep

Wandering sheep slowly meander out of the church, drawn away by other activities or interests. The drift might result from a busy travel schedule, from an unwise choice about kids' sports that takes the family away from Sunday worship, or from purchasing a fixer-upper house that consumes the weekends. Sometimes a younger member goes to college, backslides, and doesn't come back to the church or the Lord. At other times, people complain about feeling out of place in the church, so they stop showing up.

Regardless of the circumstances, these members have failed to heed the exhortation in Hebrews: "And let us be concerned about one another in order to promote love and good works, not staying away from our worship meetings, as some habitually do" (Heb. 10:24–25). They have forgotten that church membership means regular connection with other members in order to promote "love and good works." One might argue that such a wandering sheep, one who strays away from our worship meetings, is not that bad. But in fact, such a sheep is sinning by disobeying this command from Scripture.

Elders, take notice of members with overly full lives and lovingly remind them not to crowd out congregational fellowship and worship.

Limping Sheep

Jesus never promised us immunity from pain and suffering. Christians get laid off from jobs, dumped in relationships, diagnosed with type 2 diabetes, rear-ended on the highway, and hit with lawsuits. Once-active believers age and become homebound. These suffering members are limping sheep who are in danger of getting left behind because they can't keep up with the flock. They need someone to slow down and walk with them. Acute hardship can overwhelm even the stoutest saints with despair and sap their ability to maintain normal links with the church. If Job, the man of unmatched patience and faith, had his limits, so do your people.

When you know that a member is weathering a major life storm, it's time to tune in. Is that brother or sister supported by other members, whether friends or members of a Bible study? Are there practical needs that the deacons could address? Has news of the member's tribulations made it into the prayer bloodstream of the congregation? As elders, we can often serve a struggling member best by alerting and mobilizing the body even as we are reaching out ourselves to provide prayer and counsel.

It's amazing how much limping sheep savor even the smallest gestures of concern. A quick hug and a prayer in the church foyer after the service, an encouraging note, or a short visit can bolster a hurting member to keep pressing on for another month. Just last week, I asked a woman in our congregation about her husband. He has had major health issues that sometimes keep him from worship. This sister updated me on his status, then went on to praise one of our elders who had taken time to visit them. That one simple house call had lifted their faith and given them strength to persevere.

Every little bit counts. As the Lord brings wounded members to your attention, reach out.

Fighting Sheep

You will probably find this hard to believe, but I have learned there are churches where members become embroiled in conflict with one another. Of course, this has never happened in my church, and I'm sure members never fight in yours. If your church is like mine, all the members share identical views about politics and worship music, all the committees approach problem-solving and finances the same way, and no one sins against anyone else. Can you relate?

Neither can I. In fact, given the diversity of personalities and backgrounds among our members, coupled with our on-going propensity to sin, I am amazed we have as much church harmony as we do. It has to be the work of the Holy Spirit.

When church members do lock horns, as inevitably happens, there is major danger of straying. People start disappearing fast. "Church shouldn't be like this," they say. "I can't worship anymore because of all the tension I feel. I'm out of here."

Tussling members need to be challenged to make peace for God's glory and for the sake of the gospel, but they likely need help doing that. Even the most mature disciples may require a referee. Paul called out a fracas between two of his coworkers: "I urge Euodia and I urge Syntyche to agree in the Lord" (Phil. 4:2). Then he pleaded with the church to help: "Yes, I also ask you, true partner, to help these women who have contended for the gospel at my side" (v. 3).

Elders, don't turn a blind eye to strife between members in hopes that it will fix itself. It rarely does. You may be tempted to avoid and ignore, because you're a normal person who doesn't enjoy breaking up fights. But remember the words of Jesus: "The peacemakers are blessed, for they will be called sons of God" (Matt. 5:9). Grab hold of that blessing. Invite feuding members to talk with you and see what God might do. Remember, an elder's goal is mature sheep (see chapter 2). Conflicts present incredible opportunities for people to grow in Christ.

Biting Sheep

But what if the member's beef is with you, the shepherd-elder? What if the sheep nip at you when you try to get close? How are you supposed to keep watch over someone who sees you as the reason he wants to bolt?

The answer to that question can vary dramatically depending on the circumstances and the specific people involved. However, regardless of the specifics, here are three things an elder should always do when coming under scrutiny:

- Ask a few other elders to help you work with the frustrated member. As we'll see in chapter 6, this is one of the reasons God decreed that there should be more than one elder in each church, a practice we call "plural eldership." Elders keep watch over one another, because the shepherds are still sheep themselves. Humble yourself by submitting to the loving audit of other elders. If the member is out of line, let the other elders vindicate your position.
- Guard your heart from defensiveness, anger, and dismissiveness. When you reach out to other elders, don't use that as a

pretext for circling the leadership wagons. Work to sustain love and compassion toward your detractors.

- When you meet with your disgruntled sister or brother, listen carefully. I have found over the years that even my most angry, merciless critics usually have a point. It may be an overstated point, expressed in immature and sinful ways. But they are still usually responding to *something* I need to face.

KEEPING WATCH: A GOSPEL-SHAPED CALLING

Tracking down stray members in these situations is probably one of the most difficult, least glamorous parts of being an elder. You get kudos and respect from the church when you teach a class. You experience deep satisfaction from praying for members and exhilaration when you are part of an elder team that makes a historic leadership decision. But what are the personal benefits from confronting an adulterer or sticking your nose into a long-standing squabble? And who really wants to sit down and listen to an angry couple detail all the ways they believe you and the church have wronged them? Don't we all have too much drama in our lives already? Why jump into someone else's mire?

Here's one reason: elders profoundly embody the gospel when they search out wandering members. Keeping watch and tracking down strays is a Jesus-shaped activity.

The Good Shepherd came into this world to seek and save the lost. The Lamb of God came to die for unrepentant, sinning sheep like us. The Great Physician came to bind up limping sheep, sick and broken by sin. The Prince of Peace waded into our war-torn world, ripped apart by rivalries and divisions beyond number. And when we hurled insults at him, struck him, and pierced him, he did not open his mouth.

Jesus didn't have to come, but he did. And when elders take the initiative to insert themselves, even though it costs them, they exemplify the very gospel that they preach.

5

LEAD WITHOUT LORDING

The situation was deteriorating. The senior pastor and the associate pastor did not see eye to eye on several critical issues, including theology and the best approach to church ministry. Their differences were spilling out through their sermons into the congregation. The growing tension was starting to fracture the church.

After the associate pastor laid out the situation to me, I asked, "Doesn't your church have elders?" He confirmed that it did. I continued, "So what steps are they taking to resolve the conflict?"

"That's the frustrating part," he told me. "They don't know what to do. They're sending mixed signals. Sometimes they say they want me to stay on staff, but other times they seem to think that my differences with my boss are too great."

I could feel for everyone in the situation. My heart ached for two pastors who both loved the Lord but had very different views of ministry. And I sympathized with those elders. They were probably good men who wanted to serve the church, but found themselves embroiled in a complex, potentially explosive dispute between their pastors, both of whom they wanted to honor. No wonder they seemed paralyzed. Wasn't this kind of mess above their pay grade?

Yet precisely what the pastors, and the church, needed was elders willing to wade into a tangled situation and lead.

SAYS WHO?

It might seem superfluous to devote a chapter to the topic of leadership in a book about elders. Isn't it obvious that elders lead in the church? Perhaps. But sometimes we lose sight of the obvious when things get crazy.

Elders can easily feel under-qualified to lead their churches, especially during intense situations. They begin to think: "I don't have a seminary degree. I'm not trained in church management. With my busy family and full-time job, I don't have the bandwidth to tackle this problem. To be honest, I feel like nothing more than a glorified church committee member." Who are lay elders to reconfigure a church's long-standing foreign-missions philosophy, guide a congregation through an expensive facility expansion, or sort through allegations of impropriety against a staff member?

Church members might wonder, too. Sometimes a member plays along with lay elder leadership so long as the elders guide the church in a direction the member likes. But when the elders take the "wrong" fork in the road, the member balks. "Who does he think he is?" the member complains. "I was in a Bible study with him for ten years. He's no better than me. And now suddenly he's calling the shots?"

We could even step back further and question the legitimacy of elder authority within the broader context of our cultural moment. Here in the West, people tend to view leaders with suspicion. We love to question authority, build conspiracy theories, and blow whistles. The bigger the leaders are, the harder they fall—and the louder the world rejoices. As authority has shifted from external institutions to internal intuitions, each person has become his or her own sovereign. Given this atmosphere, who is an elder, let alone a church, to tell anyone how to live or what to believe?

Do elders really have authority to lead in the church?

AUTHORIZED TO LEAD

Let's start by reviewing the three interchangeable names given to this role in the New Testament. Though these three titles carry slightly different connotations, they all contain the idea of authority and leadership:

- *Elder.* This term implies wisdom and experience. You go to an elder for counsel and guidance. Elders have moral authority; when they talk, people listen.
- *Pastor/Shepherd.* Shepherds have charge over flocks, and they lead sheep from place to place. Can you imagine a shepherd who didn't care which way the flock wandered?
- *Overseer.* This term describes someone who watches over things or people.

Also, consider again a few of the texts we've studied already. As you reread these verses, notice that in each one the writer assumes the church's overseers bear authority to lead the church, and that church members have a responsibility to honor and submit to that authority:

> If anyone does not know how to manage his own household, how will he take care of God's church? (1 Tim. 3:5)

> The elders who are good leaders should be considered worthy of an ample honorarium, especially those who work hard at preaching and teaching. (1 Tim. 5:17)

> Now we ask you, brothers, to give recognition to those who labor among you and lead you in the Lord and admonish you, and to regard them very highly in love because of their work. (1 Thess. 5:12–13)

> Obey your leaders and submit to them, for they keep watch over your souls as those who will give an account. (Heb. 13:17)

Elders manage, lead, admonish, and keep watch over members. Members respond by recognizing them, regarding them highly, and obeying them.

Churches differ over how to organize themselves. Congregationally governed churches like mine don't structure themselves the way that Presbyterian churches do. Neither of us embraces an Episcopal system with bishops and archbishops like our Anglican friends. But all churches should at least agree on one thing based on the Bible's teaching: God has clearly delegated a measure of authority to elders to direct the affairs of local congregations.

LOUNGING AMONG THE LUGGAGE

If you are an elder, step up and work hard at leading your church. You don't need to have all the answers, and you certainly won't get everything exactly right. But Jesus has commissioned you to guide his flock. Your church needs you to take the initiative and plot a course forward.

You may be tempted to respond like King Saul. Though God chose Saul, and though Samuel anointed him king, Saul hid among the baggage when the time came for his national debut. It must have been a great hiding spot, because the people had to ask God where he was: "They again inquired of the LORD, 'Has the man come here yet?'" So God ratted him out: "The LORD replied, 'There he is, hidden among the supplies'" (1 Sam. 10:22). Brother elder, don't hide when the church needs leadership. It's time to crawl out of the duffle bag, exit the cargo hold, and take your seat in the cockpit.

My congregation has been blessed time and time again by courageous lay elders who provided needed leadership at key moments. I think of John, who deftly navigated us through a constitutional revision just a few years after a painful church split. His constitutional rewrite received a unanimous congregational vote. I've sat with Tim in a number of tense meetings, watching him patiently and calmly defuse feuds between members and even church staff members. I remember Matt bringing unity to the church by clearly and winsomely explaining our need for a building expansion. I'm grateful for Rick and Clay, who helped to pilot us through a complex pastoral search process. We ended up with a fantastic associate pastor. The congregation probably doesn't realize how much Eric has done for them with his relentless challenge for the other elders to be shepherds of the members.

Even as I write this, I praise God for Bill. He's currently between full-time jobs and is using his spare time and expertise in operations and team management to help me shepherd our church staff. And he's coaching me in leadership at the same time. Bonus!

I could fill the rest of this chapter with names and stories from my personal elder hall of fame. It has been a privilege to partner with men who loved this flock enough to make hard decisions, establish gospel-shaped policies, toil for church unity, persevere through setbacks, and sacrifice hours for the congregation in meetings, conversations, and prayers. Authority wielded by godly, loving men brings life, unity, and fruitfulness to local churches. And churches benefit themselves when they honor that authority (Heb. 13:17).

POWER TRIPPING

Maybe you're still not convinced.

Does all this talk of elder authority make you nervous? Even with the biblical proof texts, do you have hesitations? Maybe in your experience, the problem with elders is not that they're too much like Saul when he camouflaged himself as a supply crate in order to duck the throne. The problem is that they are more often like Saul later in his career, when he lobbed a spear at David out of jealous fear that the boy from Bethlehem would usurp his crown (1 Sam. 18:9–11). Maybe you feel the real threat is not elder timidity but elder tyranny.

I know a young Christian man who wanted to serve a local church. It was a smaller congregation that could have bene-fited from his gifts. But this young believer ran into a wall: one of the church's elders. This elder had helped to found the church, and his word carried authority. Furthermore, he sometimes wielded that authority in a very direct manner. He was one of the "bosses" of the congregation, and he wasn't afraid to let you know it. Unfortunately, the elder didn't like what this young man had to offer the church or the changes the man wanted to make. In fact, the elder wasn't a fan of changes in general. When the dust settled, the young man quietly made his exit, bruised and disillusioned.

It only takes a run-in or two with controlling, big-deal elders to make a person skeptical of terms such as "pastoral authority" and "spiritual watch-care." After all, aren't those terms that cult leaders throw around to keep people in line?

LEADING WITHOUT LORDING

Jesus and the apostles shared your concerns. They not only authorized elders to lead, but they also radically recast leadership as humble, sacrificial service to the followers. Peter affirmed the elders' responsibility to oversee and shepherd (1 Pet. 5:2), but in the same breath he called for elders to lead in a meek, exemplary manner, "not lording it over those entrusted to you, but being examples to the flock" (v. 3).

Peter might have been recalling what Jesus taught him and the other disciples about true authority and greatness in God's kingdom:

> You know that the rulers of the Gentiles dominate[1] them, and the men of high position exercise power over them. It must not be like that among you. On the contrary, whoever wants to become great among you must be your servant, and whoever wants to be first among you must be your slave; just as the Son

of Man did not come to be served, but to serve, and to give His life—a ransom for many. (Matt. 20:25–28)

When the Good Shepherd laid down his life for the sheep, he not only ransomed them from sin, he redefined greatness and authority for his ransomed flock.

At the Last Supper, Jesus stunned the disciples by washing their feet. Then he explained his shocking action this way:

So if I, your Lord and Teacher, have washed your feet, you also ought to wash one another's feet. For I have given you an example that you also should do just as I have done for you. I assure you: A slave is not greater than his master, and a messenger is not greater than the one who sent him. (John 13:14–16)

That night, Jesus stripped down and washed the dirt from the disciples' feet with his own hands. The next day, he was stripped again, and those same hands were nailed to a cross in order to wash the sin from his disciples' souls. Those who stand forgiven at the foot of the cross look at leadership and greatness in an upside-down way that scandalizes the world.

STRUCTURING FOR SERVANT LEADERSHIP

How can elders maintain the posture of humble, towel-clad foot washers and not slip into the mode of arrogant, crown-wearing despots? Can elders really lead without lording and exert authority without authoritarianism?

You can never completely eliminate the danger of overbearing leadership. Pride constantly stalks our hearts, and it is ultimately the responsibility of each elder to crucify his ego daily by the Spirit's power. But churches can also do things to foster a culture of humble governance. The leaders and the people can structure their life together in ways that make servant leadership seem normal and imperious rule seem incongruous.

Consider these six corporate habits that can help elders and congregations serve one another the way Jesus served us:

Choose Humble Elders

The simplest and most effective thing a church can do is to develop an intentional process for screening potential elders, and then be sure to select humble men. As we saw in chapter 1, the qualification lists for elders stipulate that the men must be "gentle, not quarrelsome" (1 Tim. 3:3) and "not arrogant, not hot-tempered" (Titus 1:7).

I heard a pastor say that the most important characteristic for a church leader is humility. He went on to identify the second most important characteristic: humility. The third? You can probably guess.

When choosing elders, look for men who have a track record of operating in the church with a firm but gentle hand. Servant-hearted men installed as elders will likely continue to act like servants. Even if they get a little cocky, they tend to respond well when confronted. Find men who can both speak their minds in elder meetings and also cheerfully submit to the will of the team when their positions are outvoted. Humble elders can submit to one another.

But if a man is self-important and supercilious, pigheaded and domineering, don't make the mistake of handing him a shepherd's crook, regardless of the other talents, experiences, or resources he might bring to the job: "Don't be too quick to appoint anyone as an elder, and don't share in the sins of others" (1 Tim. 5:22).

Delegate to Deacons

Elders are not the only officers in the church: the apostles also appointed deacons. At the risk of oversimplifying their job description, deacons nurture church unity by caring for the logistical, administrative, and physical needs of the church. Many view "the seven" in the early church as deacon prototypes. Their mission was to oversee the distribution of food to the church's widows so that the congregation might enjoy harmony and the apostles might be free to preach and pray (Acts 6:1–7).

Developing a healthy, empowered diaconate broadens the authority and ownership in the congregation and so creates a structural guard against elder bottlenecks of important matters. The elders still direct the affairs of the church and ultimately bear a measure of responsibility for everything in it. But they can charge deacons with certain duties and turn them loose. When elders hand things such as the church's hospitality, nursery, facilities, bookkeeping, benevolences, and technology over to qualified deacons, they communicate a humble trust in the congregation. The deacons, in turn, unburden the elders so that they can teach, pray, and shepherd, just like the "seven" did for the apostles in Acts 6.

Remain Accountable

Does your church have a process for confronting an elder who falls into sin? Paul told Timothy to hold elders in high regard

(1 Tim. 5:17–18). But in the very next verses he commanded that elders found guilty of sin should be publicly called out:

> Don't accept an accusation against an elder unless it is supported by two or three witnesses. Publicly rebuke those who sin, so that the rest will also be afraid. (1 Tim. 5:19–20)

Elders, if you find a fellow overseer walking in disobedience to the Lord and unwilling to repent, don't turn a blind eye just because he's an elder. As Paul goes on to say, "I solemnly charge you before God and Christ Jesus and the elect angels to observe these things without prejudice, doing nothing out of favoritism" (v. 21).

Honor the Word

An elder can lead without lording by keeping God's Word and the gospel central in the church. An elder should put himself continually *under* the Word—in all his teaching, worship, and ministry. This reminds both him and the congregation that his authority is contingent, and that the Bible alone is absolutely authoritative in a church's life. Congregations should select as elders men who hold the Bible itself (and not necessarily *their take* on the Bible) in highest esteem.

After all, elders bear authority over Jesus's church only to the extent that they teach, obey, and enforce Jesus's Word. As the nineteenth-century pastor William Johnson put it, elders are executives, not legislators.[2] Their job is merely to proclaim and carry out biblical teaching in the life of the church. When elders elevate the Bible, they simultaneously humble themselves. In doing so, they show themselves to be the kind of men whom true believers want to follow.

Replicate Yourself

We saw in chapter 3 that elders need to perpetuate the church's teaching ministry by training up replacements. Who will make up the next generation of teachers and elders? In addition to perpetuating the church's leadership, focusing on training helps elders stay humble. It's pretty hard to hoard power while simultaneously releasing it to others.

Trust the Congregation

I hesitate to make this point since not everyone reading this book is a congregationalist as I am. Neither is this book arguing for congregationalism. But may I humbly observe that giving the whole congregation final authority in certain areas (which even Presbyterian churches do) offers the best structural protection against elder tyranny? Having to bring major decisions before the church for approval forces the elders to let go of power and humbly trust the members and the Lord. There have been times when I wished I could make a major decision by fiat. The congregational process tends to be slower and sometimes doesn't lead to the outcome I want. But over the years, I have grown to appreciate the way that congregationalism, when practiced well, builds unity and trust between elders and members. Believing that the final authority on certain decisions rests with the congregation forces the elders to work harder at teaching and communicating with the people, and trusting God through prayer.

SHEEPY SHEPHERDS

Jesus has appointed elders as under-shepherds for his flocks. Elders should take this assignment to heart and courageously govern their churches. Wimpy, passive overseers only cause church problems to degrade from bad to worse. I plead with all my fellow elders: for the sake of the church, for the sake of the gospel, and for the sake of God's glory, lead your congregations!

But in the mist of all this shepherd-speak, remember a complementary truth: you are still sheep yourselves.

This is the great paradox that every elder faces. He is simultaneously a shepherd and a sheep, a leader of Jesus's followers and a follower of Jesus, an overseer of the local body while also a dependent part of the body. An elder is a sinful man, saved and sustained by grace, following the Good Shepherd, Jesus Christ. Suddenly Jesus turns to him, shoves a shepherd's crook into his hand, and says, "Feed My lambs" (John 21:15).

How do you resolve the inherent tension of being a sheep-turned-shepherd? You don't. You embrace it. You answer the call to shepherd and at the same time declare your utter dependence on the Lord. You say, "Let's go this way," while joining the rest of the church in crying out, "Lord, guide us." You fix your eyes on Jesus and, by his grace, lead without lording.

6

SHEPHERD TOGETHER

I am glad you're still reading this book. Frankly, I was worried you might have given up by now. Not that this has been a long book or a challenging read. Rather, I was concerned that you might have been discouraged when you saw all that the Bible requires of elders, and so dropped the book.

The opening chapter on elder qualifications was bad enough. The apostles set a high bar for elders: Christlike character, a well-managed home, and an ability to teach and defend biblical truth. And what about being "above reproach"? Anyone in touch with his faults and weaknesses would find that profile sobering, to say the least. As I wrote that chapter, I couldn't help but reflect, "Am I *really* qualified to be an elder, let alone to write a chapter on elder qualifications?"

But even if you squeaked past the initial screening, the weighty duties in chapters 2 through 5 could have finished you off. Elders pastor a flock, teach doctrine, refute error, nurture the members toward maturity, track down strays, govern and lead, and defuse conflicts, to name a few of their duties.

And we still have three chapters to go.

This job description overwhelms me at times, and I'm a paid pastor who devotes my entire workweek to the task. But what if you're a lay elder with a demanding job, a grinding commute, an active family, a house to maintain, and maybe even a hobby or two? How can you do justice to the high calling of congregational oversight in the limited hours you have to spare? It feels like a formula for failure. Is lay shepherding really possible?

I believe it is. Part of the solution lies in embracing and sacrificially prioritizing your call to shepherd. Alexander Strauch has some straight talk for us:

> Many people raise families, work, and give substantial hours of time to community service, clubs, athletic activities and/or religious institutions. The cults have built up large lay movements that survive primarily because of the volunteer time of their members. We Bible-believing Christians are becoming a lazy, soft, pay-for-it-to-be-done group of Christians. It is positively amazing how much people can accomplish when they are motivated to work for something they love. I've seen people build and remodel houses in their spare time.[1]

Aspiring elders should count the cost of serving and then spend themselves liberally for their churches while trusting in God's grace.

But there is another factor that makes lay shepherding sustainable. It's one of the elements of biblical eldership that has kept me going strong as a pastor over the years. When God designed the local church, he wisely put in place a *plurality* of elders. Shepherding is possible because it is supposed to be a team sport.

PASTORING IN THE PLURAL

When the New Testament describes actual elders functioning in churches, it speaks about them in the plural. Scan the following verses. Notice that multiple elders lead each individual church:

> When they arrived at Jerusalem, they were welcomed by the church, the apostles, and the elders. (Acts 15:4; see also vv. 6, 22; 16:4)

> When they had appointed elders in every church and prayed with fasting, they committed them to the Lord in whom they had believed. (Acts 14:23)

> Now from Miletus, he sent to Ephesus and called for the elders of the church. (Acts 20:17)

> Paul and Timothy, slaves of Christ Jesus: To all the saints in Christ Jesus who are in Philippi, including the overseers and deacons. (Phil. 1:1)

> The reason I left you in Crete was to set right what was left undone and, as I directed you, to appoint elders in every town. (Titus 1:5)

> Therefore, as a fellow elder and witness to the sufferings of the Messiah and also a participant in the glory about to be revealed, I exhort the elders among you. (1 Pet. 5:1)

> Is anyone among you sick? He should call for the elders of the church, and they should pray over him after anointing him with olive oil in the name of the Lord. (James 5:14)

Do you see the pattern? Again and again we find elders (plural) in each church (singular).[2] Each congregation had its own pastoral squad. It is an elementary observation, but it makes all the difference when you put it into action. Elder plurality is extremely significant for sustainable shepherding.

SHARE THE LOAD

Start with the obvious: having multiple elders spreads out the pastoral workload. "Many hands make light work," "Teamwork divides the task and multiplies the success," and all those other proverbs prove true for elder ministry.

A member of our church once asked me how she could pray for me. I shared about the growing burden of the ministry. Our church membership had been increasing at that time, and the pastoral needs had multiplied. I asked her somewhat rhetorically, "How do I minister effectively to a growing flock?"

She didn't take my question rhetorically. I'll never forget her answer. She smiled, shrugged, and simply said, "More shepherds."

Of course—more shepherds. I couldn't believe I hadn't thought of that before.

Well, I suppose if Moses could miss the obvious, so could I. His father-in-law, Jethro, had to pull him aside and point out his need for more help.

> The next day Moses sat down to judge the people, and they stood around Moses from morning until evening. . . . "What you're doing is not good," Moses' father-in-law said to him. "You will certainly wear out both yourself and these people who

are with you, because the task is too heavy for you. You can't do it alone." (Ex. 18:13, 17–18)

And what was Jethro's solution? He advised partners in the work:

> "But you should select from all the people able men, God-fearing, trustworthy, and hating bribes. . . . They should judge the people at all times. Then they can bring you every important case but judge every minor case themselves. In this way you will lighten your load, and they will bear it with you." (Ex. 18:21–22)

Just as adding judges relieved Moses, so having multiple elders distributes the weight of ministry. So if you're an elder, find ways you and your colleagues can parcel out the work. Communicate about the hot spots in the church that need attention and coordinate your efforts. If you are overwhelmed, don't just keep gutting it out—shoot up a distress flare and call in brothers for help.

How might you more intentionally disperse responsibilities among your overseer team? I've mentioned how our elders have attempted to divide up the church membership among them, but you don't have to do it that way. The point is to be intentional about sharing the work.

SWISS ARMY ELDERS

The benefits of shared shepherding don't stop with a division of labor. Plurality also enables a church to access the diverse gifting among the elders so that each one operates out of his strengths. Although all the elders bear the same responsibilities, they bring an assortment of talents and experiences to the mix.

I remember getting my first Swiss Army knife as a kid. I can't recall exactly how old I was, but I can still picture the shiny red grips on the outside of the knife. And tucked in between those grips were the signature Swiss Army tools themselves. I remember the excitement of folding out the tools one by one and imagining how I might use each to stay alive while lost in the wilderness. There was a longer knife, a shorter knife, tweezers, a screwdriver, scissors, and, of course, that most critical of outdoor survival tools, a corkscrew.

I get a similar feeling each year when we welcome new men onto our church's elder board. Each brother brings unique gifts to the team that beg to be discovered and used. It's like opening a human Swiss Army knife, one elder gift at a time. Of course, all elders should share some gifts that are basic to the role, such as leading and teaching. Yet even those gifts can vary in strength and shape.

On our current elder team, Mark is an adjunct professor at a local seminary who uses his pronounced speaking gifts and advanced New Testament studies to exercise a powerful teaching ministry within the congregation. Time and time again, Kent has leveraged his career in finance to provide leadership on our budgeting issues. John has a deep passion for prayer and has called our somewhat pragmatic elder team back to its knees many times over the years. Herb has uncommon common sense and usually asks a penetrating question during a discussion that brings us to the nub of an issue.

Take time to learn about your fellow elders. Figure out what gifts each one carries folded up in his life and learn how to draw them out. When you work together, you may become frustrated at the different ways some of the other overseers solve problems or set priorities. But don't let yourself get annoyed by those differences. Instead, see the other elders as part of the divinely engineered tool set for serving your congregation. It's all part of the genius of elder plurality.

SHEPHERD THE SHEPHERDS

In the last chapter, we were reminded that elders are also members of Jesus's flock. We called it the "sheep-as-shepherds" paradox of church leadership. This paradox raises an interesting question: If the shepherds are simultaneously sheep, who shepherds the shepherds? Elders need pastoral care just like everyone else. They can give in to temptation, succumb to depression, become embroiled in conflicts, grow weary in church ministry, or lose loved ones. Even if they're not in a crisis, elders need to continue maturing, just like every other church member. Who oversees them spiritually?

Here again, plurality provides an answer. The shepherds must shepherd the shepherds. Congregational oversight is sustainable because the elders, in plurality, act as pastors to one another.

Several years back, a brother joined our elder team for the first time. I said half-jokingly to his wife, "Are you ready for the trials?"

"What trials?" she asked.

"The trials that will come upon you and your husband when he becomes an elder. Get ready to be tested," I replied.

Apparently I jested better than I knew. He lost his job while serving as an elder and remained unemployed for more than a year. During that "involuntary sabbatical," the other elders poured a steady stream of prayer and encouragement into his life. By God's grace and their support, he came through that season stronger and more refined.

If you're an elder, take a risk and get real with the others. Don't be afraid to reveal your hurts and fears, your struggles and sins. The other elders can't pastor you well if you pretend to be Superman. Specifically, ask them to pray for needs in your life. As I mentioned earlier, our elders gather twice each month, with one of those meetings devoted to prayer. At that prayer meeting, we ask how we can pray for each other. It's a little practice that helps us stay attuned to one another's sheepy side.

At one elder prayer gathering many years back, when we asked how we could pray for one another, one of the elders took off the proverbial mask. He spoke candidly about a crisis in his business and finances, and his resulting struggle with despair. It was a raw moment, but it opened a door. A few of the other elders stepped through that door and shared about needs in their marriages. Our subsequent prayer time that evening was anything but perfunctory. We interceded for one another with new fervor and compassion.

If you're going to pastor a congregation effectively, you need to be under spiritual oversight yourself. So humble yourself and allow the other elders to care for you.

SHARPEN THE IRON

We've been considering how plurality makes pastoral work sustainable, especially for lay elders. A team approach promotes better pastoring because it protects elders from exhaustion by distributing the ministry load, pools complementary talents and gifts, and supports elders in their trials.

But there is another constellation of dangers for shepherds: pride, control, heavy-handedness, unapproachability, and even abusiveness. As we saw in the last chapter, elders must lead without lording. Plurality helps to guard against our domineering tendencies by creating a context in which elders can put into practice that famous proverb, "Iron sharpens iron, and one man sharpens another" (Prov. 27:17).

When elders are practicing a healthy plurality, it's harder for one man's views or tendencies to dominate, because the elders offset one another. The gentler elders temper the more fiery ones. The activists move the analyzers toward actually making decisions. The big-faith elders keep every decision from being one more exercise in fiscal conservatism and risk management, while the practical elders help the dreamers and visionaries not to do stupid things under the pretext of "trusting God." That sort of mutual balancing generates an atmosphere that's hard for egotists to tolerate.

But even more to the point, plurality creates a structure for elders to call one another out when one of them gets off track.

Our elder meetings occasionally get heated. (I realize that doesn't happen in *most* churches, so you may need to use your imagination.) Our congregation happens to be blessed with strong leaders who hold strong opinions, many of whom serve as elders. When challenging issues arise during elder meetings, so can the temperature in the room.

Yet I have been touched again and again to see elders pull one another aside after a meeting. Sometimes a man apologizes to another for coming on too strong. They might grab coffee later that week and talk through their differences. At other times, a brother challenges another on his conduct during the meeting and urges him to make amends and change his approach. Younger elders have gently pushed back against the veterans when those older elders dominated conversations in ways that silenced the younger ones. Overseers have stood up in church meetings to apologize to the congregation for the tone of their responses in previous meetings, thanks to the gentle urging of their fellow overseers.

One elder has always been outspoken. On the one hand, it is great to have him as an elder because he helps us to not fall into groupthink, thanks to his ability to articulate opposing viewpoints with passion. I have come to appreciate this about him more and more, especially since I tend to avoid conflict. On the other hand, that outspokenness can generate friction. Still, he has been known to call me after an elder meeting and ask if he crossed a line or if an apology is necessary. If I say, "Yeah, you might have been a little harsh," this elder immediately takes steps to make things right. Over the years, I have witnessed him become more gentle, tactful, and sensitive without losing his gift for forthright speech.

ENJOY THE RIDE

Let me make one final pitch for elder plurality. It is much more satisfying, and even fun, to pastor as a team than to be a lone-wolf shepherd. Looking back on more than a decade and a half of pastoral ministry, I can say that one of my greatest ministry joys has been serving with the lay elders of my congregation. These men have been a band of brothers for me and for one another. We have shared laughter and tears. We have celebrated victories together and prayed our way through seemingly unsolvable conundrums. They have stood by me, sometimes quite literally, during some of the hardest moments of my ministry. Many times, I have led them well. At other times, they have picked me up and carried me until I could lead again.

If you are in a church with a solo paid pastor and no other elders, I plead with you to use whatever influence you have to move your church toward adopting lay overseers. Not only is your mono-pastorate biblically out of order, but your present structure also robs your pastor of vital support and deep satisfaction. It also deprives the other church members of richer pastoral care, as well as the joy of seeing men from their number blossom as leaders. And there are men in your congregation who are missing opportunities for growth that will come only when they step out in faith to oversee a congregation.

You need elders (plural). That is Jesus's plan for sustainable, effective shepherding in his churches.

7

MODEL MATURITY

On the morning of January 1, 1996, I sat down in my office as the new interim assistant pastor of South Shore Baptist Church. Nothing conveys a sense of significance and job security like the title "interim assistant pastor."

But that morning, I was just happy to be done with school and have a real ministry job. I had finished my last seminary classes a few weeks earlier, wrapping up two and a half years of full-time graduate study. And immediately prior to seminary, I had pushed through four years of undergraduate work in biblical studies. With more than six years of uninterrupted schooling under my belt, I clearly had everything necessary to be a pastor: two theological degrees, a budding commentary collection, and a few sermons at the ready from my preaching classes. What else did I need?

There was one "small" thing I was missing: I needed someone to show me how to actually pastor a congregation.

So God gave me Ray.

The church had hired Ray to be the interim pastor a few weeks before they called me. Ray is a wise old New England minister who, over the next year and a half, showed me how to shepherd a church. I watched him navigate the strong currents of our elder board. I sat in on his pastoral counseling sessions and tagged along on hospital visits. He gave me templates for weddings and funerals that I still use today. I got to see good pastoring in action. I sometimes joke that if I do something right in pastoral ministry, it's probably because I am copying Ray, and if I do something wrong, it's probably because I'm improvising.

But even more than teaching me ministry skills, Ray modeled the character and heart of a pastor. He demonstrated patience by bringing change at a pace slow enough for a Yankee church to handle. He exuded kindness, humility, and joy, even when he wasn't getting his way. He trusted God and solved problem after problem through prayer. And above all else, Ray loved the people, and they knew it. In the end, Ray not only showed me how to be a pastor, he showed the whole church how to follow Jesus.

IMITATE ME

My experience with Ray makes me think of what Paul told the church in Corinth: "Imitate me, as I also imitate Christ" (1 Cor. 11:1). Does that sound strange to you? Have you ever told another Christian to imitate your imitation of Jesus? It sounds like a presumptuous, churchy variant of the game "charades." Imagine yourself saying to your Bible study group or to your fellow church committee members, "I want to let you all know that I'm following Jesus pretty well, so you should probably copy me." Maybe that verse was a line only Paul could deliver. After all, he was an apostle. He could get away with saying grandiose things like "imitate me."

But Paul went further. He not only said, "Imitate me," he also urged the church in Philippi to pay attention to those who imitated him: "Join in imitating me, brothers, and observe those who live according to the example you have in us" (Phil. 3:17). Did you notice the last word in that verse? He said "us" rather than "me." The "us" in Philippians refers to Paul and Timothy (1:1). So the circle of role models expanded beyond Paul to include Timothy and the Christians in Philippi who replicated Paul and Timothy's pattern of life.

In his letter to Timothy, Paul explicitly instructed his young pupil to be a model for imitation: "Let no one despise your youth; instead, you should be an example to the believers in speech, in conduct, in love, in faith, in purity" (1 Tim. 4:12).

What if being an example to imitate is not a role reserved just for the holy apostles? What if modeling and copying are twin beats that lay down the normal rhythm of Christian discipleship? What if what we really need to grow in maturity are more Rays and Timothys setting examples in our churches?

That would make sense, given the way that God seems to have hardwired us for imitation. From infancy, we learn to speak, behave, and react by mimicking those around us. Every dad has had those terrifying moments of hearing his own words coming out of his child's mouth. Mothers worry about whom their teens will choose as friends, because they understand the power of peer modeling. Even as adults, we pick up accents, phrases, facial expressions, humor, tastes, habits, and hobbies from one another. It's why couples who have been happily married for fifty years seem to have slowly oozed together into one person.

This dynamic of model and copy, example and imitator, carries over into Christian discipleship. However, the Christian life does not *start* with imitation; it starts with a miracle. Discipleship begins when a sinner hears the gospel and the Holy Spirit supernaturally changes her inner disposition through the hearing. As a result, the sinner repents of her sin and believes that Jesus died and rose again to save her. She has been born again by God's power, and her first cry is "Jesus is Lord!" A person must be born again in order to enter God's kingdom. No one can imitate her way from unbelief to belief.

But now our heaven-born, spiritual infant must grow up into Christlike maturity. How does this happen? It involves a number of factors, such as receiving nourishment from God's Word. But she also needs something else. Our newborn child of God needs a family where she can learn by the example of others how to walk with Jesus. She needs a local church.

A healthy local church provides a rich matrix of relationships for mutual modeling and copying. By becoming a member of a gospel fellowship, our new Christian can compare notes with other newborn believers who are adapting to the strange, wonderful life of a forgiven Jesus follower. She can learn from older siblings who have followed Jesus longer and, in the process, won victories over sin through the Spirit's power and weathered some significant life storms by trusting in God's grace. She may even find a few godly mothers and fathers, like the apostle Paul and like Interim Pastor Ray, who inspire her to pray, "Lord, help me to be like that one." We need not only solid teaching and preaching about obedient Christian living, we also need to see holiness in practice. We grow through imitating, like the apostles imitating Jesus, like Timothy imitating Paul, and like Jeramie imitating Ray.

SHEPHERDING BY BEING

So what does all this have to do with elders? This book is supposed to be a job description for overseers. Where do they figure into this discussion about modeling and copying?

It's simple: God has called elders to be men worth imitating.

A healthy local church typically has many people, men and women, whose example we could follow. But when a church appoints a man to be an overseer, it is formally saying, "Here is an official, church-recognized example of a mature follower of Jesus." He is not the only example, not a perfect example, and not necessarily the best example in that congregation for every single Christian virtue. But an elder is a duly designated model nonetheless. By affirming someone as an elder, the church says, "Imitate him as he imitates Christ." A church should be able to direct a newborn believer to an elder and say: "Do you want to know what a real Christian should be like? Then look at him."

To put it another way, an elder's job involves shepherding by *being* as well as by *doing*. Elders pastor churches not only by what they do but also by who they are. And without the being, the doing falls apart.

Let's review the elements of an elder's job description that we laid out in the previous chapters. Notice how each element of this to-do list can be achieved only if the elder fulfills his to-be calling. In short, Christlike character is a *sine qua non* of pastoral ministry.

In chapter 2, we summarized the entire elder job description as shepherding church members toward greater Christlike maturity. Elders are pastors who invest in the lives of the church members in order to help them grow up together more and more into the image of Jesus.

But if an elder is immature himself, how can he possibly shepherd others toward grown-up godliness? Just as you wouldn't hire a financial advisor who had squandered his own wealth through bad investment decisions, and just as exercising with an out-of-shape fitness coach would not inspire your confidence, so an ungodly, selfish elder who says "Imitate me" has few takers. You can bring others in Christ only as far as you have gone yourself.

Chapter 3 laid out the teaching task. Elders expound biblical truth and refute doctrinal error. But what if the teacher's life contradicts his teaching in glaring ways? All but the most devoted Kool-Aid drinkers stop listening. People don't have much patience for the "Do as I say, not as I do" type of teacher. Even worse, hypocritical teachers of God's people have to face God. No wonder James warned, "Not many should become teachers, my brothers, knowing that we will receive a stricter judgment" (James 3:1).

But when a pastor combines sound teaching with sound living, he never lacks a devoted flock. When I think of Ray's teaching ministry as our interim pastor, one sermon stands out. During Easter week, Ray taught from John 13 about Jesus washing the disciples' feet. I remember that sermon for two reasons. First, it was a great sermon. Ray spoke clearly and movingly about the servanthood of Jesus, not only in washing feet but in going to the cross to wash away sins. Ray called our congregation to similar humble service to one another in light of the gospel.

Second, and maybe more important, I remember that sermon because as I listened to words about servanthood, I also saw humility, service, and self-sacrifice in the man who preached it. Ray's consistent Christian walk compelled me to listen to his message.

In chapter 4, we examined the demanding elder responsibility to track down straying members. It's a sensitive task because members who wander from the church are often fragile and hurting. As a result, they often struggle to trust others. So when a shepherd with questionable character pursues, the lost sheep likely skedaddles. How can a sheep take a shepherd's efforts to "keep watch" over him seriously when the elder cannot even keep watch over himself?

We can take it a step further. If a pastor's hypocrisy is known beyond the walls of the church, it hinders others from even wanting to pay a Sunday visit to the fold. "Furthermore, he must have a good reputation among outsiders, so that he does not fall into disgrace and the Devil's trap" (1 Tim. 3:7).

In chapter 5, we wrestled with the tension between leading confidently and yet gently. Again, godly character is the key. As Peter said, "Shepherd God's flock among you . . . not lording it over those entrusted to you, but being examples to the flock" (1 Pet. 5:2–3). Being an example is the antidote to being a bully. When elders live and love like Jesus, they aren't known for being arrogant or domineering. Instead, they possess a Jesus-shaped humility that gives them a moral authority to which the church willingly defers. Elders must lead by example if they hope to lead at all.

Finally, we discussed elder plurality in chapter 6. Overseers set an example not only as individuals but as a team. Think of your elder group as the church in microcosm. The way the shepherds interact, solve problems, strive for unity, and face challenges together should be a living dramatization for the whole church to emulate. An elder team should be able to say collectively, "Imitate us as we imitate Christ together."

I once taught a class on biblical eldership at our church. As part of the class, we took a "field trip" to a live elder meeting. Afterward, the class members debriefed together about the experience. They remarked on the love, humility, and kindness they saw the elders expressing to one another, as well as the sincere concern the elders showed when they prayed for the church members. Some in the class had expected something different from the elders in that meeting, something more high-powered, corporate, and intimidating. Instead, they found something in the elders' interactions that looked like Jesus. It was a good night for our overseers.

Can you see how the lifeblood of godliness should pulse through every task an elder does? But if an elder compromises his integrity through disobedience to the Lord, his ministry dies. An elder's walk with Jesus is the string on which all the pearls of his job description are strung. Cut that string and the pearls drop to the ground and scatter everywhere. An elder may be talented, experienced, and charismatic, but if he doesn't reflect Jesus well, his immaturity will eventually sweep the legs out from under his gifting. An elder's *being* gives credibility and power to his *doing*. That explains why the Bible has such extensive qualification lists for elders, as we saw in chapter 1, and why those qualifications primarily focus on exemplary character. An elder must be "above reproach" (1 Tim. 3:2). His whole ministry depends on it.

WATCH YOUR LIFE

Given the vital importance of elders' being examples to the church, we cannot end this chapter without adding another critical duty to the elder job description: every elder must continually pursue holiness, love, and spiritual maturity. Elders need to look more and more like Jesus in order to lead like Jesus.

Paul said this to Timothy: "Pay close attention to your life and your teaching; persevere in these things, for by doing this you will save both yourself and your hearers" (1 Tim. 4:16). That is an amazing statement and a stunning responsibility. Paul was saying that the pastor plays some God-ordained part in the salvation of his soul and those of others by paying attention to his life and teaching.

The teaching part might be less shocking to us. People are saved by means of hearing the gospel taught from the Bible, so if a church leader guards his teaching against error, then that teaching can be a conduit for God's saving grace.

But what about the shepherd's life? By paying attention to his life and being "an example to the believers in speech, in conduct, in love, in faith, in purity" (v. 12), he plays some role in his own salvation and that of the people in his congregation. God's Spirit somehow uses the well-tended life of an overseer in the outworking of salvation for others in the church. Therefore, modeling and copying are not optional. They are central to how we make spiritual progress together in the local church.

So brother elder, above all else, watch your life. If you hope to say along with Paul, "Imitate me, as I also imitate Christ" (1 Cor. 11:1), then you must first join him in declaring, "I discipline my body and bring it under strict control, so that after preaching to others, I myself will not be disqualified" (1 Cor. 9:27).

Know your soul and your disqualifying propensities. Be aware of the low spots in your heart's wall, where temptations tend to make their assaults. Continue to fight back against sin and kill it by the Spirit's power wherever you find it (Rom. 8:13). Keep in step with the Spirit (Gal. 5:16) so that the deeds of the flesh might wither and the fruit of the Spirit ripen (vv. 19–23). Let God's Word renew your mind so that you can continually put on the new self (Eph. 4:22–24). Daily offer your body as a living sacrifice (Rom. 12:1–2).

MAKING GOSPEL PROGRESS

Don't assume that because you are an elder you have finally arrived. It's just the opposite: becoming a church overseer should inject you with a new urgency to go further in your own imitation of Jesus.

Your congregation needs to see not only a godly elder, but a growing elder. Paul told Timothy not only to pay attention to his life, but also to make public improvement: "Practice these things; be committed to them, so that your progress may be evident to all" (1 Tim. 4:15). Isn't that interesting? Your congregation needs to see progress, not perfection. Jesus already has perfection covered. The church needs to imitate not only the degree to which you have grown in Christ, but also, and just as important, the fact that you are still growing.

In other words, the church needs to see the gospel still transforming your life. The sheep need to know that you too regularly repent of sin. They need to hear you crying out in prayer for Jesus's resurrection power in your soul. They need to know that you read the Bible and pray every day, not because you are the church's designated super-saint, but because you have learned that without a daily serving of manna you don't have strength each day to resist temptation or to serve the Lord.

By modeling gospel-dependent progress, you point church members beyond yourself: you lift their gaze to Jesus, the One into whose image we are being transformed.

8

PLEAD FOR THE FLOCK

Over the last seven chapters, we have explored the biblical job description for elders. In attempting to summarize that job description, we have said that it is about shepherding church members toward greater Christlike maturity. However, we could also say that elders are called to *shepherd local churches like Jesus.*

An elder's labors follow many of the patterns of Jesus's ministry to the disciples. Jesus taught God's Word; elders continue to teach that same Word. Jesus came from heaven to seek and save the lost; elders, similarly, track down the strays, sometimes at personal cost. Jesus perfectly embodies the image of God; elders seek to imitate Jesus in a way that makes them examples to church members. Elders shepherd churches like Jesus by teaching, leading, pursuing, serving, and modeling like Jesus.

But we're forgetting something. Elders must also emulate the other "half" of Jesus's ministry. Shepherding like Jesus means praying like Jesus:

> But the news about Him spread even more, and large crowds
> would come together to hear Him and to be healed of their sick-

nesses. Yet He often withdrew to deserted places and prayed. (Luke 5:15–16)

These verses provide a summary of Jesus's ministry up to his passion. We're familiar with the first half of the summary, his public ministry, because the Gospels spend a lot of time describing it. Again and again we see Jesus teaching, working miracles, and ministering among the people.

But what about the other half of the summary, the part that describes how Jesus "often" withdrew by himself to pray? We don't know as much about that aspect, mainly because the Gospel writers don't go into as much detail about Jesus's prayer life. But if we pay attention, we can catch repeated glimpses of this understated yet integral dimension of Jesus's ministry. Let's stay with Luke's writings:

- Jesus prayed at his baptism, at which point heaven opened, the Spirit descended, and the Father spoke (3:21–22).
- Jesus started a busy day of ministry in Capernaum by going to a deserted place, presumably to pray (4:42; cf. 5:16).
- He spent the entire night outdoors praying before he chose the twelve apostles (6:12).
- Jesus prayed in private with the disciples (9:18), and even took Peter, James, and John up on a mountain to pray, which is when they saw him transfigured (9:28).
- Jesus's example of intercession prompted the disciples to ask him to teach them to pray (11:1), so he gave them the Lord's Prayer.
- He told the parable of the persistent widow in order to inspire them "to pray always and not become discouraged" (18:1).
- Mere hours before his crucifixion, Jesus fended off temptation in Gethsemane by pleading with the Father (22:39–44).

- In Luke's sequel, the book of Acts, the apostles were "continually united in prayer" after Jesus's departure (1:14).
- As the church was born and grew in size, the apostles discovered that caring for the congregation's practical needs squeezed out time for prayer. So they proposed appointing seven men to tackle the church's growing administrative needs (6:1–3). What would the apostles do with the reclaimed time and energy? They said, "We will devote ourselves to prayer and to the preaching ministry" (v. 4).

The apostles carried forward Jesus's pattern, a two-pronged ministry of preaching and prayer.

Does it seem strange to you that the apostles, and even the Lord Jesus, devoted so much of their energies to praying so intentionally? Does conversation with the Father mark your life and ministry the way it did those of Jesus and his apostles?

LIVING ON A PRAYER

Our practice of prayer not only needs to be pulled forward by the template of Jesus's personal communion with the Father, it also should be pushed ahead by the demanding nature of shepherding work itself. Pastoral ministry can bring you to your knees, one way or another.

I hope that at this point you have a healthy trepidation at the prospect of overseeing a congregation. The work can be grueling. Teaching, mentoring, confronting, pursuing, and leading people takes significant time and can be soul-wearying. And no matter how much pastoring one does, there is always more that could be done. An elder could always make another phone call, disciple another person, or invite someone else over for a meal. How does a shepherd define the word *done*?

It's no wonder elders easily regress to the trustee model. It is much easier to sit around a table for a few hours, discuss a few policies, and take some votes. "Done" is when the meeting adjourns. But when you lean into pastoral ministry to people, whether you are a paid staffer or a lay overseer, you come face to face with the limitations of your time, energies, knowledge, and gifting. Hopefully, that confrontation drives you to cry out for God's help. For elders, prayer is not just a duty, it's a crucial survival strategy.

But it is not only the scope of the work that should shove elders toward prayer, it is also the goal of the work. As we saw in chapter 2, elders aim toward maturing church members in Christ, yet they have no power to make anyone else progress spiritually. Overseers can teach the Bible, but they cannot make people obey it from the heart. An elder can exhort fighting members to be reconciled, but he cannot make either party forgive. God has given elders a goal that only God himself can bring to pass. As Paul reminded the shepherd-worshiping Corinthian church: "I planted, Apollos watered, but God gave the growth. So then neither the one who plants nor the one who waters is anything, but only God who gives the growth" (1 Cor. 3:6–7).

Our spiritual inability should drive us to call out for God's power to bring growth to our congregations. Like Elijah, we can repair the altar and prepare the sacrifice, but God must send down the fire of his Spirit into people's hearts and lives (see 1 Kings 18:30–39).

If the demanding scope and humanly impossible success criteria of an elder's job description are not enough to send him pleading to heaven for help, one glance in the mirror should do it. Any elder with an ounce of self-awareness knows that his own proclivities to sin can scuttle his ministry. He opens the Bible and sees his heart reflected in Abraham's deception, David's lust, Elijah's despair, Hezekiah's pride, and Peter's betrayal. And if that weren't bad enough, he reads that there is a lion who prowls about with a hankering for lamb (1 Pet. 5:8). When an elder realizes he is a thirsty, wounded, wandering, hunted sheep himself, he will bleat for the Good Shepherd's aid.

Yes, Jesus's example pulls us elders to pray. But the demands of pastoral ministry and our own deficiencies should also push us to ask Jesus to do the impossible. Overseers not only pray in order to shepherd like Jesus, we pray because we need Jesus to do the shepherding through us and to us. An elder's ministry lives on prayer.

PRACTICING PRAYER

What does prayer-soaked elder ministry look like? How do elders inspired by Jesus and made desperate by their responsibilities turn up the prayer volume?

Try not to think of prayer as an extra activity tossed onto your already overloaded schedule. Rather, think of it as the operating system on which all of the elder apps run. As Paul said, "Pray constantly" (1 Thess. 5:17). Prayer is at its best when it is the verbal overflow of a steady state of dependence on God. Just like character, prayer should flow through everything an elder does. It should be a kind of regular spiritual respiration that brings the Spirit's life to our lives and labors.

Here are four possible approaches for weaving intercession into the fabric of your elder work.

Public Prayer

Try to use any moment of public leadership as an excuse for prayer. Be a prayer opportunist. Whether you are officiating the Lord's Supper, teaching a Sunday school class, speaking at a ministry training seminar, or moderating a church meeting, take advantage of your authority in that moment to pray on behalf of the group gathered with you. When you are with other church members in some group problem-solving activity, be the guy who says, "Perhaps we should pause and ask God for help." If you ask any gathering of your congregation if you can pray, no one will *ever* object.

In addition to the value of prayer itself, infusing intercession into public assemblies also gives you an opportunity to teach people how to pray by modeling it. So when you are praying on behalf of assembled members, try to demonstrate heartfelt, balanced prayer. Be sure to pray not only for individual needs in the congregation, but also for other churches and for the planting of new churches in your region. Don't pray just for the upcoming election in your country, but lift up the work of the gospel globally. Pray for daily bread, but don't forget to plead for God's kingdom to come and his will to be done. And try to start your prayers the way most of the prayers in the Bible start, namely, by exalting God's character and deeds: "Hallowed be thy name"! (Matt. 6:9, kjv). By God's grace, the people will imitate your prayers as you imitate biblical patterns.

When you pray publicly, you not only model how to pray, you also exemplify an attitude of dependency. If the spiritual leader says, "We need God's help," he sends a powerful message to the followers. Dependent public prayer is a yet another way of leading without lording.

When I was in seminary, I studied under a professor named Meredith Kline. By the time I took his class, he was almost ready to retire. Dr. Kline was admired for his scholarship in the area of biblical theology. He had a passion for understanding and explaining how the whole story of the Bible fits together. But it wasn't just his comprehensive theological framework, which helped me read my Bible as a unity, that impacted me: Dr. Kline affected me by his praying.

He started every class with prayer. He had a dry, raspy, somewhat quiet voice, poorly suited to the task of interceding publicly. And he gave *long* prayers. Dr. Kline would often pray for ten minutes or more. Yet his conversation with God was riveting. During his prayer, it was as if he turned his vast knowledge of the Bible and theology into worship and awe for God. I saw a towering intellect humbling himself before the greatness of God, savoring the length and breadth of God's saving work in Jesus. That little old man stirred my heart in class with a desire to know and talk to God the way he did. He used his public platform as an opportunity for public prayer to great effect in his students' lives.

Few elders or pastors have the scholarly depth of Dr. Kline. But all church overseers have public venues that can be graciously hijacked for heartfelt, biblical prayer. And it doesn't require a PhD.

Presbyter Prayer

Make prayer part and parcel of your "presbyter meeting" (*presbyter* is yet another word for *elder*). It's time to evolve beyond merely asking someone to "open" and "close" the meeting in prayer. Block out time for extended intercession together whenever you meet. In fact, make it the first item on the meeting agenda.

Also, feel free to interject impromptu prayers as you move through the meeting. I appreciate how Bob has done this in our elder meetings. At times, we have to discuss heavy topics, such as a heartbreaking situation involving a church member or a difficult decision that must be made without black and white options. Bob often raises his hand and says, "Can we stop for a moment and pray about this?" Making tough decisions is one of those elder apps I mentioned above, but dependent prayer is the operating system.

One simple way to transform your elder meetings, and your fellow elders, is to pray systematically through your church's membership list together. When you do so, not only do your members receive the inherent blessings that come from someone praying for them, but you and the other elders refocus yourselves on the church's members rather than on its machinery. The elders may even find interceding for members more satisfying work than debating how much to spend on a new heating system or whether to allow the town garden club to hold an event in the church's facility.

Here's how the elders in my church have tried to put all of this together. I offer this as one possible way to structure prayer in your elder meetings, but certainly not the only or even the best way. Our elders meet formally twice each month. We have a "prayer" meeting on the first Tuesday and a "business" meeting on the third Tuesday. We try to pray at our business meetings, too, though not as extensively.

At the prayer meeting, we share known needs in the church, including our own needs as elders, then we spend the rest of the time praying for those requests and praying through a chunk of the church membership list. The elder prayer meeting is probably one of our all-time favorite church activities.

A final thought: consider calling your fellow elders to special seasons of prayer, and even fasting. When our elders have faced difficult moments in our church's life, we have occasionally set aside a week for fasting and prayer. Different elders are assigned fast days so that the whole week is covered. We need to do it more often.

Personal Prayer

By "personal" prayer, I don't mean praying by yourself (we'll talk about that next under "private prayer"). I mean person-to-person prayer with members.

Again, this praying is not another activity to add to your elder to-do list. Rather, it should be part of your regular shepherding work. Whenever you talk to a church member, try to pray for him or her, right then and there, in person. Take whatever things you have talked about together and lift them up to God, whether you're meeting with someone over coffee or talking after a dinner at your house. Even if you're standing in a busy church lobby after a Sunday gathering and a member shares a concern or trial, try stopping right there and asking, "Can I pray about this right now?" I have never had anyone decline.

Also, figure out a way for your elder board to put James 5:14–15 into practice:

> Is anyone among you sick? He should call for the elders of the church, and they should pray over him after anointing him with olive oil in the name of the Lord. The prayer of faith will save the sick person, and the Lord will restore him to health; if he has committed sins, he will be forgiven.

Those verses raise lots of interesting questions, such as, "Do you have to use oil?" "What is the relationship between sickness and sin?" and "How does elder prayer for the sick relate to forgiveness?" My goal here is not to give a detailed interpretation of this verse. Rather, it's simply to ask, "Do you and your fellow elders ever pray over sick people like James says?"

Our elders have taken up this practice, and many have said it is one of the highlights of their elder ministry. We have seen God work. Sometimes God has given sick members a measure of relief for a time. In some instances, God appears to have granted miraculous healings, the kinds that make oncologists scratch their heads in befuddlement. At other times, I'm not sure whether God has done any healing in the body, but the sick member has been spiritually fortified to press on.

As I write this, my father is battling cancer. He and my mother are members of the congregation. They asked the elders for prayer, and the elders came and prayed for him. We don't yet know how God will answer that prayer for healing. But I will say that the experience of having almost a dozen godly men in my parents' living room pouring out their hearts to God for Mom and Dad was a profound moment for my parents, and for those men.

Private Prayer

Finally, it is imperative that you block out time for private intercession and communion with God. Hopefully, by this point, your desperate need for private prayer as an elder is unavoidably plain. If you don't walk closely with the Lord yourself, you will wander from the path and maybe take the sheep with you.

Be intentional about baking private prayer into your life. Set aside time daily, somewhere, somehow. Pray during your commute, when you walk the dog, or when you run an errand. Carry a membership list with you and remember each person before God in spare moments.

Private prayer and fellowship with Jesus through his Word may be among the most neglected habits among pastors. Yet, ironically, these are arguably the most determinative practices for spiritual vitality in our lives and ministries. What would happen in our local flocks if Jesus's under-shepherds gave themselves to prayer the way they give themselves to budgets, e-mails, and policies?

JOIN THE PRAYER MEETING

We started this chapter by ruminating on Jesus's practice of prayer. Prayer saturated and propelled his public ministry.

Elders should look at the model of Jesus (and the apostles) and long to emulate him.

But there's another aspect to Jesus's prayer ministry we should keep in mind: Jesus is still praying.

Jesus is alive and sitting at the Father's right hand, interceding for his people as our high priest (Rom. 8:34; Heb. 7:25). Jesus our advocate speaks to the Father in our defense (1 John 2:1). Mere hours before he went to the cross, Jesus prayed that the Father would protect the disciples from falling away like Judas (John 17:11–15). And his people continue to be kept by God's grace as Jesus converses with the Father on our behalf.

So when elders pray for their churches, they aren't just imitating Jesus, they are joining Jesus. The under-shepherds combine their voices with the Chief Shepherd himself in asking the Father to guard the sheep and bring them safely home.

CONCLUSION

The Eternal Weight of Shepherding

Serving as an elder in a local congregation is an immense privilege and responsibility because it carries an eternal significance. The task seems daunting, even impossible at times. Yet it is worthy of everything you pour into it, because you are stewarding nothing less than the blood-bought people of God and working for their eternal good and God's eternal glory.

So to fellow and would-be elders, let me leave you with two final thoughts in light of this eternal weight of shepherding. One is a warning and the other is a promise.

First, the warning: *Shepherd well, because there is an account to be given*. Remember the words we studied in Hebrews:

> Obey your leaders and submit to them, for they keep watch over your souls as those who will give an account, so that they can do this with joy and not with grief, for that would be unprofitable for you. (Heb. 13:17)

This text primarily admonishes church members, but there's a warning for overseers nestled into it. Elders keep watch "as those who will give an account." The church belongs to Jesus. He bought the sheep. Elders are mere caretakers of those "entrusted" to them (1 Pet. 5:3). Pastors will answer to the Owner himself for how we handle his flock. We will answer to the Groom for how we treat his bride. Do we teach his truth, his whole truth, and nothing but his truth? Do we love his sheep the way he loves them? Are we abusive or humble? Do we point our brothers and sisters toward Jesus or do we act as stumbling blocks as they try to follow him?

But there's an eternal promise as well: *Shepherd well, because there is a crown to be gained.* After Peter exhorted his fellow elders to humble, exemplary shepherding, he gave this promise: "And when the chief Shepherd appears, you will receive the unfading crown of glory" (1 Pet. 5:4).

So much of what we work for and worry about each week is vapid. Ecclesiastes reminds us that our toil and accomplishment is vanity. We amass and build, only to leave it to others. But the reward for productive shepherding never spoils. What else do you do every week that promises an unfading crown?

Brothers, as you consider being an elder and count the cost, remember to factor in the eternal glory in store for good and faithful servants.

> Many of those who sleep in the dust of the earth will awake, some to eternal life, and some to shame and eternal contempt. Those who are wise will shine like the bright expanse of the heavens, and those who lead many to righteousness, like the stars forever and ever. (Dan. 12:2–3)

NOTES

Introduction: "I'm an elder. Now what?"

1 I am using the word *lay* in the basic sense of "volunteer" or "unpaid." I am not using the word to suggest a clergy vs. laity distinction. On the contrary, this book will argue that an unpaid elder and a paid pastor or minister occupy the same role, even if the congregation has chosen to pay the latter so that he can give more hours to the task.

2 Notice how the words *elders, overseer, shepherd,* and *overseeing* are used interchangeably in the following texts: Acts 20:17, 28; Titus 1:5–7; 1 Peter 5:1–5.

Chapter 1: Don't Assume

1 Thabiti Anyabwile, *Finding Faithful Elders and Deacons* (Wheaton, IL: Crossway, 2012), 57.

2 It seems unlikely the phrase was intended as a prohibition against polygamy since the inverse of the phrase, "a one-man woman," is used to describe widows who qualify for church charity (1 Tim. 5:9), and there was certainly no practice of polyandry in the Greco-Roman world. Ruling out polygamy, the phrase must then be taken either (1) literally, to mean having never been remarried, whether divorced or widowed; or (2) figuratively, perhaps to mean something like "being a faithful spouse." I lean toward the latter interpretation. For a fuller discussion, see George Knight III, *The Pastoral Epistles: A Commentary on the Greek Text* (Grand Rapids: Eerdmans, 1992), 157–58.

3 I realize this is a hotly contested issue, and unfortunately I'm able to gesture only briefly toward a few arguments in support of my view. For a thorough handling of the relevant texts and issues, see Wayne Grudem, *Evangelical Feminism and Biblical Truth: An Analysis of*

More than 100 Disputed Questions (Colorado Springs, CO: Multnomah, 2004).

Chapter 2: Smell Like Sheep

1 For a helpful discussion of this concept, see Alexander Strauch, *Biblical Eldership: An Urgent Call to Restore Biblical Church Leadership* (Littleton, CO: Lewis and Roth, 1995), 45–50.

2 See Colin Marshall and Tony Payne, *The Trellis and the Vine: The Ministry Mind-Shift That Changes Everything* (Kingsford, NSW, Australia: Matthias Media, 2009).

Chapter 4: Track Down the Strays

1 For a great introduction to church membership, see Jonathan Leeman, *Church Membership: How the World Knows Who Represents Jesus* (Wheaton, IL: Crossway, 2012).

Chapter 5: Lead without Lording

1 Interestingly, the Greek word for "dominate" here in Matthew 20:25 is the same one that Peter uses (1 Pet. 5:3). Besides those verses, the word occurs in Mark 10:42 (a parallel text to Matthew) and Acts 19:16.

2 Cited in Mark Dever, ed., *Polity: Biblical Arguments on How to Conduct Church Life* (Washington, DC: Nine Marks Ministries, 2001), 195.

Chapter 6: Shepherd Together

1 Alexander Strauch, *Biblical Eldership: An Urgent Call to Restore Biblical Church Leadership* (Littleton, CO: Lewis and Roth Publishers, 1995), 28.

2 Ibid., 37.

GENERAL INDEX

SCRIPTURE INDEX

9Marks

Building Healthy Churches

9Marks exists to equip church leaders with a biblical vision and practical resources for displaying God's glory to the nations through healthy churches.

To that end, we want to see churches characterized by these nine marks of health:

1   Expositional Preaching
2   Biblical Theology
3   A Biblical Understanding of the Gospel
4   A Biblical Understanding of Conversion
5   A Biblical Understanding of Evangelism
6   Biblical Church Membership
7   Biblical Church Discipline
8   Biblical Discipleship
9   Biblical Church Leadership

Find all our Crossway titles
and other resources at
www.9Marks.org

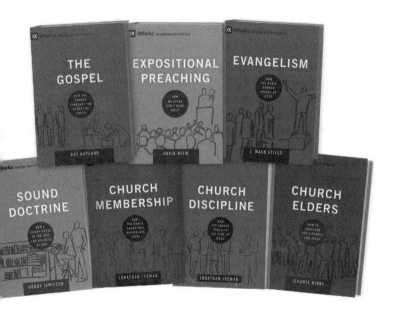